HIGHWAY SIGNS *and wonders*

40 Years of Miracles and Ministry on the Road

by Thomas Dorland Cobb

Thomas Dorland Cobb
89616 Rockford Bridge Road
Merriman, NE 69218

All scripture quoted is taken from the
King James Version
unless otherwise noted

First printing, September 2011

ISBN: 978-0-9650711-2-3

Published by *Sword and Vine Books*
a division of *Life Unlimited!!* ministries

Printed at
Service Press
P.O. Box 606
Henderson, NE 68371

CONTENTS

Eleven years ago, I wrote a book which I entitled *Highway Signs and Wonders*. As it turned out, it sold pretty well and in a few months I needed to reorder more copies. I didn't do it, however, because by that time I had decided to make some changes in the manuscript.

About three months ago, after all these years, God told me it was time for me to rewrite it. I've gone back over it, discarded the unnecessary parts, and I've added several chapters telling about the "signs and wonders" we've experienced over the last ten years. I really believe you'll find inspiration and will enjoy my "new and improved" version of *Highway Signs and Wonders*.

Chapter One

From the Sandhills to the Shenandoah

I wonder if Abraham felt like this. My vision for the future was similar to his. I had left my familiar Nebraska Sandhills to embark on a journey that would take me to places I had never been before. I would have no permanent dwelling but would follow, day by day, the path God laid out before me. Instead of living in a tent as Abraham had, my family and I would be living in RVs.

It seemed a perfect morning. Although the sun would be rising soon in the east, a full moon still reflected its light from the west on the Virginia highway. The long shadows of tall poplar trees punctuated the glistening roadway with darkness as I steered the motor home to our destination. In the distance, the Blue Ridge Mountains silhouetted the horizon. The dim moonlight revealed enough of the lush landscape as I navigated the narrow winding road through the Shenandoah Valley that I felt I had somehow been transported to the Garden of Eden. It certainly didn't look anything at all like the wild sandhills and soap weeds of Western Nebraska.

It was four o'clock in the morning. Everyone, even Kiley, was asleep. The continual droning of the engine of the Dodge Travco motor home and the uneventful expanse of highway we were traveling had finally lulled everyone to sleep. I could hear Kenneth's snores emanating from the bunk directly behind me and if I looked over my shoulder, I could see Karen's graceful form in her bunk. Directly beneath her our sound equipment was stacked in a pile on my bed. The stillness in the other upper bunk directly behind my head, above Kenneth, assured me that my little daughter was finally sleeping peacefully.

My hopes, dreams, ambitions, and even what I felt was my calling all seemed to materialize before me in the predawn hours of the morning. I was in the process of accomplishing at that moment what had only a few months before seemed impossible. I was responding to Christ's commission, found in Mark's Gospel: *"Go into all the world and preach the gospel to every creature. "* (Mark 16:15) The time had come for me to add my efforts to the millions of others who were still trying to bring this commission to fulfillment. As I was driving along, I pondered this commission wondering why nearly two thousand years had gone by and it still had not been fully carried out. Why hadn't the Christians just gone out and done what they had been told to do? Why was the world still so unaffected by the message of the gospel? I understood my own shortcomings and had no problem explaining why I, personally, seemed to be so ineffective. Yet I knew of many other people that had so much to give. I could see no reason why I couldn't help those who did have God-given talents. The least I could do would be to offer my services to the people who had the ability to get the job done.

That was the mind-set that had brought my family and me halfway across America. I was part of a group, seven of us in all who would travel the nation sharing the love of God to all who would listen. I anticipated that one day we would draw larger crowds than even Billy Graham. The lesser members of the team would prepare the hearts of the people by sharing music and leading them in praises to God. The audience would then be more receptive and ready to receive the message that our leader, Paul Secord, would share with them.

Paul was one of the best preachers I had ever heard and it seemed that whenever he preached there was always some kind of positive response. Although they were native Virginians, Paul and his wife, Mahala, had previously lived in South Dakota while they traveled for a few years in a ministry team called the Lundstrums.

I had been a fan of the Lundstrums from the first time I had heard them. Late one evening as I was turning the radio dial looking for a Christian station, I heard an unfamiliar country song with words that weren't about someone losing his wife, lover, pickup truck, or dog; instead it was a song about Jesus. I had stumbled onto the Lundstrum's program called Message for America. I was a brand-new, born again believer with a great amount of enthusiasm and a million questions about my new-found faith in God; and I was thrilled to hear Lowell Lundstrum answer some of those questions in his radio sermon.

The Lundstrum's approach was to blend a modern style of country gospel music with an intense evangelistic message. They were well known throughout the Great Plains of Middle America and were notably successful. When they spent about five days sharing their ministry in Valentine, Nebraska (the largest town in my home county) they drew crowds of thousands of people. Cherry County encompasses an area as large as the state of Connecticut, yet the population of the entire county is less than six thousand. The Lundstrums, however, claimed nearly a thousand converts during their crusade in Valentine.

That kind of results and that proportion of success, if repeated elsewhere and in larger population centers, could certainly affect the entire nation and even the world. To me, their approach seemed to hold the key to fulfilling Christ's commission. Being from South Dakota, they related well to

7

the farmers and the agricultural communities of the Midwest and Western plains; but sadly, they didn't seem to have the same impact on the metropolitan areas of our nation. From my viewpoint, however, it seemed that the very thing that caused their success in rural areas — their simple, straightforward, down-home country manner — was their biggest drawback when they tried to minister in the cities. Big city people seemed to need someone with a different cultural style.

Paul, it appeared to me, was the very person who could do it. He was raised in Manassas, Virginia, on the outskirts of Washington D.C., and was the son of a popular Assembly of God evangelist. He was an outstanding musician, trained at the Conservatory of Music in Winchester, Virginia. He understood the big city mentality and seemed to be in touch with its fast pace. He also knew the Lundstrum's formula for success. Why not take what was working for them and apply it to the people that he could relate to?

Prior to this time, whenever the Lundstrum's made appearances anywhere close to my hometown I would gather my wife and baby and drive wherever they were performing to see them in person. Over the years, I had gotten personally acquainted with both Lowell and Paul. During one of their performances at Pine Ridge, South Dakota (about 75 miles from my home), Lowell made an announcement that Paul, his piano player, would be leaving the team soon to start his own ministry out on the East Coast.

As soon as I found an opportunity, I approached Paul to learn more about his plans. It was at that time when he shared with me his vision for reaching the East Coast using the approach he had learned from the Lundstrums. His brother-in-law, Kenneth Snyder, and his wife Mahala, would make up his team. He hoped, however, to add more personnel later on if things went well enough for them. "What type of personnel are you looking for?" I asked, a bit hopeful that I might find a place to use my particular talents.

"I'd really like to have a lead guitar player, and perhaps someone to play another keyboard -- maybe an organist." Paul replied. It was hard to believe what I had just heard. It seemed to me that my wife and I were exactly what he was looking for.

* * * *

When I was just a boy, I began learning to play the guitar. I was the youngest in my family and even before I became a teenager I could play well enough to become part of the family country-western band that my father had put together. When I was in high school, a few of my friends and I formed our own rock-and-roll band.

After high school, I married Karen Hoffman, my high school sweetheart. Karen began playing the piano when she was only seven. She was installed as her church's organist when she was fourteen. After we were married, she learned to play the bass guitar and the both of us joined a country-western band, playing almost every Friday and Saturday night. I was trying to get into the ranching business by then and we needed the extra money we made from playing in dance halls and bars to pay our bills.

Then, in the spring of 1968, my wife and I became born again Christians. It immediately became important for us to find and follow the will of God in every area of our lives. My limited exposure to the Christian realm in our narrow corner of the world didn't seem to include our particular taste in music — at least not in those days. That was why I

9

was so excited when I discovered the Lundstrum's program on the radio. Their music was a style we enjoyed and the message was one I felt God could bless. I desperately wanted to become a part of it.

* * * *

Even though I could think of a dozen reasons why such an ambition might never actually become a reality, I asked Paul if he would let me audition for a position with his group. I hadn't brought my guitar with me to the Pine Ridge crusade, so I got Lowell's permission to use his guitar and played a few licks for Paul as a demonstration of my abilities. Both Paul and Lowell seemed impressed by my audition and Paul promised to stay in touch and let me know how things were going with his new group out on the East Coast. If things worked out as well as he planned, perhaps a year or two later he'd be ready for some extra personnel.

It was about six months later when I got a call from Paul telling me that things were going much better than he had ever hoped. Their itinerary was nearly booked solid, they had released their first record album, and best of all, they would be coming through our area on their way to other engagements. They had a few days left open, however, and they hoped they could spend this time with us to get better acquainted.

The fact that Paul and Mahala wanted to get to know us better seemed a pretty fair indication that they were seriously considering having us join their group. If this was indeed the case and we actually did join them, it would be the biggest adventure and most notable change of our lives.

Chapter Two

Lloyd's Bible

I was raised in a community where neighbors lived miles from each other. My father was probably one of the most dedicated cattle ranchers who ever lived. More than just an occupation, ranching almost seemed to be his religion as well. Completely committed to the care of his cattle, he often risked his life and willingly sacrificed his comfort to face fierce blizzards, searing heat, and anything else that might threaten the safety or productivity of his herd. From my early childhood on, he pressed his primary philosophy upon me and my family that "the cows must come first."

"Take care of the cows," he would tell us, "and the cows will take care of you!"

Dad would tolerate our musical interests. In fact, he was proud of our accomplishments in that area; but it was understood by all of us that nothing should overshadow our ranching profession. He was very disappointed and even somewhat despondent when one of my brothers told him one day that he had decided he didn't want to be a rancher. What he really wanted to do was to go to college and become a doctor.

The rest of us were happy to conform to our father's philosophies and were grateful for the start he gave us. Shortly after Karen and I were married, he helped me make a down payment on a small ranch adjoining his. I would pay him back by working for him until I had enough cattle and land to make it on my own.

Things went along reasonably well for the next four years. Little by little, I increased the size of my herd and added to my ranch by leasing an adjoining parcel of land to help support the additional cattle. We did this in spite of the fact that Western Nebraska ranchers weren't having an easy time of it in those days. Cattle prices were not keeping pace with inflation. Land taxes and feed costs rose continually and, in order to make it, ranchers had to cut corners wherever they could. Because of this, many of my young friends and even some of our neighbors chose more promising careers and moved away to pursue their ambitions. The majority of our remaining neighbors and friends were at least twenty years older than Karen and me.

We weren't in the habit of attending church on a consistent basis, but when we did, we usually went to a little country church at Eli, Nebraska. Eli was a ghost town that began dying when the main highway was rerouted two miles outside of town during the 1930's. After thirty-five years had passed, all that remained of Eli was one general store, several old deteriorating buildings, and the Eli Wesleyan Methodist Church. The church, like the town, had seen its better days. There were only four or five families still attending there with any regularity.

The pastor of this church and his wife were one of the few people in our community that were about our age. Once in awhile when we attended church at Eli, the pastor's wife would invite Karen and me over to the parsonage for Sunday dinner. The pastor's name was Lloyd Phipps and his wife's name was Janice; but no one that I knew of ever called him Reverend Phipps, or even Pastor Lloyd. We simply knew him as Lloyd and his wife as Jan. They had one little blonde-haired baby girl named Janel.

Lloyd had been raised in a pastor' home, so his interests usually concerned things other than cattle and horses. Often our conversation around the dinner table was about current affairs and local happenings. One particular Sunday the topic of conversation was about Israel. It was in 1967 and the nation of Israel was under attack from Egypt and its allies. Its army and air-force vastly outnumbered, it appeared that Israel's days as an independent nation were about to come to an abrupt end. Since these events were the headlines of the day, it was only natural that our conversation turned to the prospect of Israel's uncertain future.

Lloyd confidently stated, as if he already knew what would shortly transpire, "I wouldn't worry too much about Israel if I were you. It's Egypt and the other nations I would be concerned about. They're about to suffer one of their greatest defeats ever!"

"Why do you think that?" I asked, a little surprised that Lloyd would make such a wild prediction when it was obvious that Israel was in very deep trouble.

"I've already read about it in the Bible," he replied. "Once Israel became a nation in 1948, she will never again cease being a nation. Wait and see." Then he added, "God will fight for her!"

I was skeptical of Lloyd's confidence, but intrigued with the concept that this young pastor actually believed he could predict the outcome of this modern war by studying the pages of Scripture. By the following Sunday I was no longer skeptical. Israel's latest war was over in just six days! The armies of her enemies lay in shambles on the Sinai desert and Israel's future as a nation appeared to be more secure than ever, just as Lloyd had predicted.

* * * *

As a rancher's son, I learned early in life that there is a

certain etiquette that cowboys are supposed to follow concerning their conversation and it was rare for any self-respecting cowboy to violate it. First of all, one was never to ask another rancher how much land he owned or how many cattle he had. Such information was considered too private and personal to reveal. Only someone unfamiliar with our culture would ever violate this rule.

Second, sex was a taboo issue. Cowboys might swap dirty stories with each other by the hour and no one cared if they laced their talk with profane and obscene words, but a person's personal sex life and practices were not to be discussed. I don't recall my father ever sitting down when I was a young man to tell me about "the birds and the bees". It would have been far beneath his dignity to do so. On the other hand, there really wasn't a need for him to discuss the topic. I had a pretty good indication about these things when we turned the bulls out to pasture with the cows every year in the early summer. I suppose my father must have decided that I could figure out just about everything I needed to know on my own.

Thirdly, religion was a subject that was every bit as personal and private as sex. It was impressed upon me, at a time before I have any recollection, that it just is not right for one person to pry into another person's spiritual affairs. Also, it was an embarrassment for someone to bare his spiritual condition to another. It was something that just wasn't done in my family. I would no more be inclined to ask my father about his relationship with God than I would ask him about his sex life.

Lloyd, of course, had no such inhibitions about religion or discussions about his own or someone else's spiritual condition. It was always awkward for me whenever these issues came up. One thing that I found fascinating, however, was Lloyd's own matter-of-fact relationship with God. He would refer to conversations he had with his Heavenly Father as if they were actually two-sided. In fact, he acted upon the instructions that he claimed to receive continually, in a manner similar to my obedience to my own father's instructions.

What impressed me most of all were the stories he shared about God's provision. He had, for example, enrolled in Bible College with little more than the shirt on his back. Yet he supported himself, paying for his college tuition and books almost entirely by faith. He graduated four years later with every bill paid and entirely debt-free. For him every day was a continual adventure as God performed one miracle after another — and each miracle seemed specifically designed for his personal benefit. I had never met anyone with such a close relationship with God. Until then, I thought the only people who had actually lived that way were the special individuals told about in the Bible.

When Lloyd shared his secret of success with me, I was surprised at its simplicity. All he did, he claimed, was search the Bible for promises and then believe them once they had been revealed. He emphasized that the key to all of this was God's Word. He assured me that God would never violate His own Word.

With this particular understanding of the Bible, I was naturally drawn to the Word to find out for myself what it actually said. To help me with this, Lloyd thought I might be more successful using an Amplified Bible and loaned me his. I began reading it feverishly, going over it chapter by chapter and verse by verse. In less than a month, I had read it from cover to cover. I spent almost every evening after work in my bedroom listening to the radio, scanning the dial trying to find a Christian program or a preacher who could help explain what I had been reading.

Lloyd's Bible was a prized possession of mine and I took it with me wherever I went. I even carried it with me in a saddle bag when we used our horses to sort cattle or drive them from one pasture to another. One afternoon Karen and I were out in a pasture on our horses, miles from any shelter, when a thunderstorm suddenly appeared on the horizon. The fast-moving storm blew in upon us and we had no choice but to weather it as best we could. Rain came down in torrents for awhile and we tried to shelter ourselves by standing down-wind behind our horses. By the time the storm was over, we were soaked to the skin. I had endured such downpours in the open pasture before and was used to being soaking wet, but what concerned me now was Lloyd's Bible. I had no doubt that the fragile onion-skin paper of its pages was ruined. Reaching into the saddle bag which was still half-filled with water, I pulled out a completely dry Bible! Karen and I marveled at this honest-to-goodness miracle. This was the kind of thing Lloyd had been telling us about. It served as a special confirmation to me that his stories were actually true. God, we discovered, was not impersonal and far away after all. He still performs miracles in every generation and His promises are relevant for each and every day.

Chapter Three

Taxation, Salvation, Procreation

The winter of 1968-69 wasn't an easy time for us. Feed costs were high, the winter was hard, and our taxes, especially our property taxes, were getting harder and harder to pay.

I was happy to see the ice beginning to thaw on the Niobrara River in early March. It was an indication that spring would be coming soon. *Perhaps this depressing winter,* I thought to myself, is *finally about over!*

There were a few cows stranded on the wrong side of the river. They had wintered there since the river had frozen in December. The steep hills that ran down to a small clearing on the north side of the river gave the cattle protection from the cold northern winds. The snow didn't usually collect on the hills, and that left tufts of grass available for the cattle to feed on. We supplemented their welfare by driving our pickup to the top of the north hills every few days — as close to the cattle as we could get — and rolling fifty-pound protein blocks down the steep embankment for them to feed on. Considering their isolation they had survived pretty well; but now that the river ice was melting it was time to bring them home.

I wasn't sure if I was doing the right thing or not. *I wonder if it would be better,* I speculated, *if I waited a few more days before trying to cross the river after the water settles down a little more.* On the other hand, it was such a nice day for this time of year and it probably wouldn't stay that way for very long. If another blizzard rolled in, which would be typical for early March, I may not have another opportunity for several more weeks to drive the cattle across the river.

The sand on the river bottom was bound to be loose and "quick" because it had only been a few days since the ice had melted. The kind of quicksand I was concerned about wasn't the kind you see in the movies when someone slowly sinks in the mire until they pass out of sight. Rather, it was the kind where a horse or cow sinks in up to its belly and the sand hardens around its feet pinning it in place. I had seen animals that had died, stuck in the sand, trapped only a few feet from the river bank. They did not die from drowning or starvation but from exhaustion as they struggled to free themselves from their entrapment. The interesting thing about the sand was this: if you were to ride across it quickly, keeping your horse moving so the sand didn't have time to set up around the horse's legs, you would leave a path of hard moist sand which could then be traversed safely. I intended to cross the river several times, punching holes in the sand, leaving a passage that I could drive the cattle across.

The river was shallow and wide at this particular crossing, only about four feet at its deepest point. The extra width of the river, however, made quite a long distance that my horse had to cross. It was exhausting work for her to keep pulling her feet from the sand which continued to harden around each forward footstep. We were halfway across at the river's deepest point when my horse finally stumbled and fell on her side into the water. I went down with her, still seated in the saddle, falling between the horse and the oncoming current. The force of the water washed me back under my horse and pinned me there. As tired as she was, it would normally have been her natural instinct to lay still in the water allowing the force of the river's current to flush her out of her trap, floating her downstream to more shallow water. If she would have done so, I would certainly have drowned, since I was still pinned in the saddle beneath the water.

With the weight of the horse holding me down, I fought to get free or at least to obtain a breath of fresh air. Just when I felt I couldn't stand it any longer, my horse suddenly began struggling to regain her balance and get back up on her feet. Temporarily released from her weight, I was able to reach the surface and take a few gasps of air. I had only a few seconds to do so until the horse lost her balance, falling down upon me and entrapping me all over again. I remained pinned under the water for about the same amount of time as before until the scenario repeated itself. Once again I enjoyed a few moments of fresh air as the horse struggled to get back on her feet. Then down she came again, her weight and the river's current both tearing me away from my next breath of air.

How long will she keep this up? I wondered. It seemed as if she was teasing me, giving me brief moments of hope punctuated by eternities of despair. I was aware that time was not on my side. Eventually, I reasoned, *she'll be too tired to struggle anymore and she'll have to rest for a longer period of time than I can take.*

Suddenly, she seemed jolted by a fresh burst of energy and with a violent jerk, sprang to her feet and regained her balance. I was free at last! Turning around in the water she retraced her steps, walking back across where the sand had now become firm. I followed her to the river bank and laid down on the dry ground nearly exhausted, enjoying the privilege of taking long deep breaths of air without interruption.

Wow! Am I ever lucky! I thought to myself. Somehow it never occurred to me to thank God that I was still alive.

A few days later I told Jan, Lloyd's wife, about my narrow escape.

"It sounds like God has something special in mind for you! She exclaimed.

"Me?" I responded. "What possible interest would God have in me?"

Late one evening a few weeks later, I as seated at my desk paying bills and trying to catch up on a few other matters of business. One of these items was my personal property tax form. The State of Nebraska required all professional farmers and ranchers to list the number of cattle and horses they owned, grain and hay crops still in their possession, an assessment of the value of their machinery, and almost everything else connected with the operation of their businesses. We were required to pay an annual tax based on the value of these possessions. Overwhelmed by so many bills and the prospect of still more to come, I began contemplating ways to cut corners.

It doesn't seem fair, I thought to myself. *The state assesses my taxes according to the number of cattle I own, not by their actual value. It doesn't matter to them whether my cow is worth two hundred dollars or two thousand dollars. I have to pay the same rate of tax on my little two-year-old heifers — which are worth only about two hundred dollars —as some of the big-shot ranchers around here pay on their registered Hereford cows — which may be worth two thousand dollars! How would they ever find out how many cattle I own, anyhow? They don't even know where I keep them all.*

I had almost decided, rather than list everything I owned, that I could save money if I shaved the actual number of my herd by about twenty-five percent. I was in the process of calculating my figures accordingly when I suddenly recalled a passage of scripture that had apparently been stored away in the recesses of my mind without my awareness. I heard a voice from within my spirit that seemed independent from my own thoughts saying, "What does it profit a man if he should gain the whole world and lose his own soul! What shall he give in exchange for his soul?"

I recognized the message and realized that it came from the bible. I had heard a preacher refer to this passage when I attended church as a child — but it had never affected me this way before.

I picked up Lloyd's Amplified Bible which was lying on the desk next to the bills and flipped through it randomly. The sixteenth chapter of Acts opened before me and I began reading the account of Paul and Silas in jail. An earthquake had shaken the cell doors open, giving Paul and Silas a means of escape. More concerned about their jailer's plight than they were of their own freedom or comfort, they assured him that they would stay where they were. Their astonished jailer then asked, "Men, what is it necessary for me to do that I may be saved?" (Acts 16:30).

Their answer, as translated in the Amplified Bible, was, "Believe in and on the Lord Jesus Christ — that is, give yourself up to Him, take yourself out of your own keeping and entrust yourself into His keeping, and you will be saved..."

I felt challenged to apply to myself what was required of the jailer — to take myself out of my own keeping and entrust my life and welfare to God. If I did, it would be an act of faith on my part because I honestly wasn't sure I could make a living, make my payments, and keep paying my bills unless I cheated on my taxes — which I felt I could justify doing since they seemed unfair anyway.

As I recalled the events of the past few weeks and how

21

God had revealed His personal interest in me, it was enough to tip the scales. I prayed, *God I'm not sure where I'm going from here — whether I'll go broke, break even, or become wealthy — but wherever I go and whatever I do, I want you to go with me!*

Feeling immense relief, I filled out an honest tax report and mailed it the next day. Subsequently, my life has never been the same.

An ongoing debate among Christians is the theological issue of whether or not, once a person obtains salvation, it is possible for him to lose it. For many the issue is still unresolved. I've talked to several Christians, however, who admit that if it is possible for people to lose their salvation, the times they've come very close to doing so may have been while they were paying their taxes. As far as I know, I'm the only person alive who actually obtained his salvation *because* of his taxes!

I was baptized shortly afterward in the same river I had almost drowned in just a few months before.

Karen accepted the Lord shortly after I did and during the next winter we were blessed to learn that Karen was pregnant. After nearly four years of marriage we were finally going to become parents. The baby was due the latter part of July. As summer arrived, Karen and I became more and more excited about the arrival of our first baby. The baby's due date was the thirtieth of July; but that day came and went with no sign of its arrival. Two more weeks passed and still no baby. In our sparsely populated community there aren't many physicians, so when our doctor decided to take a vacation and leave his patients in the care of a visiting physician who would commute from Chadron, Nebraska to the hospital at Rushville, Nebraska (thirty miles away), we started getting anxious.

On the afternoon of August sixteenth, Karen felt her first labor pain. Since we lived so far away, I immediately put her in the car and took her to the hospital where she was quickly admitted. I paced the halls like a typical first-time father expecting the baby to be born at any moment. It wasn't. Morning came and still the baby hadn't arrived. When the visiting doctor came in from Chadron that afternoon, he checked on Karen who was still having regular labor pains. Deciding the baby wouldn't arrive any time soon, he went back to Chardon. I began to worry. Karen spent another restless night, intermittently dozing between labor pains and awakening with a start each time the next one came.

Throughout the next day and on through the following night, her labor pains would become regular, increasing in intensity, getting closer and closer until they were only about three minutes apart. Then suddenly they would ease off, back to about fifteen minutes between them, becoming much more erratic. This happened for the next three or four hours — giving us hope only to be deferred over and over again. Karen and I spent most of this time walking up and down the hospital aisles, arm in arm, hoping that the physical activity would speed things along.

If a cow went this long without delivering her calf, I'd shoot her to put her out of her misery! I mused. I prayed that something would happen or that someone would do something.

On the morning of the third day, the pains became more frequent, more intense, and more consistent. By this time Karen was nearly exhausted from her long ordeal but found a hidden source of strength when she read in her Bible: "I will lift up mine eyes unto the hills, from whence cometh my help. My help cometh from the Lord, which made heaven and earth." (Psalm 121:1).

When the doctor came from Chadron on his daily rounds that afternoon, Karen was experiencing hard labor and both of us were hopeful that our baby would finally be delivered.

He glanced at Karen and then looked at her chart and casually commented to the nurse, "I don't think the baby will be coming any time soon today either. I'm going back to Chadron to finish my golf game. If something happens tonight, call me!"

The nurse stared at him in disbelief.

"Doctor are you sure? She seems to be in hard labor now!" she protested.

Unconcerned, the doctor walked down the hall toward the hospital door. Just then, Karen had the hardest contraction she had had yet. Feeling extremely weak and bearing excruciating pain, she felt a sensation with which she was totally unfamiliar. Her consciousness, at that moment, seemed to disconnect itself from her physical body and present circumstances. It seemed as if she was beginning to slip off into a different dimension of existence. She was jolted back to the horror and reality of the moment, however, when a nurse (who had detected that Karen was slipping away) slapped her on the cheeks and yelled, "Karen! Karen! Stay with us now!"

Recognizing the seriousness of the situation, another nurse ran to the parking lot and blocked the doctor's exit by standing in front of his car. "Doctor, come back!" she ordered. "We need you! The baby is coming now!"

A few minutes later Kiley, our beautiful baby girl was born. Karen had been in labor for three full days. Amazingly, both she and the baby had survived the delivery.

Chapter Four

Adventures in Faith

One day, as we were listening to the Lundstrums program on the radio, I commented to Karen, "Wouldn't that be fun to do what the Lundstrums do? Just travel around the country playing music and telling people about Jesus?"

"I prefer doing what we're doing now," she replied, somewhat sullen.

Karen, for the most part, felt fulfilled in our little isolated home along the Niobrara River. She had plenty of time to enjoy our new baby and also found contentment and purpose working in her garden, raising flowers, or picking and canning vegetables. I, on the other hand, wasn't as content as Karen appeared to be in our present situation.

I continued trying to satisfy my voracious appetite for the Word of God. I read the Bible or books about the Bible whenever I had any time at all to spare. I must have made a nuisance of myself in Pastor Lloyd's study, showing up every so often with another Biblical issue that I wanted to discuss. I didn't know much about Christianity but I wanted to learn all I could.

* * * *

During the fall, an early snowstorm covered the countryside with a fresh blanket of wet snow. Our home was located in a river valley and the only road in or out required travel up and down the steep river hill. My father had asked me the night before if I would drive up to his place in the morning to help him with his work. I hadn't expected four inches of wet snow to accumulate during the night when I promised him that I would.

I knew I had almost no chance at all of being able to reach the top of the hill in my 1953 Chevrolet pickup truck but decided to give it a try anyway. At least I could tell my dad that I had given it my best shot if he asked why I hadn't shown up for work that morning. Revving the engine on the straight stretch of road at the bottom of the hill, I took a run at it hoping to maintain enough momentum to make it past the top. I made a gallant effort, the tires spinning and sliding all the way, but the pickup finally slowed to a stop and spun out about half way up the hill.

Holding both the brake and the clutch, I was about to shift into reverse so I could back down the hill and go home when I felt something bump the back of my truck. As I was pushed slightly forward, I released the clutch and continued my climb up the hill with my pickup crawling along in low gear. I was too busy steering and making sure I didn't slide into the ditch to look behind me, but I was certain my neighbor who also lived in the river valley had come up from behind in his four-wheel-drive unit and was helping me by pushing me up the hill. When I finally reached the hill's crest and my pickup regained enough traction to make it the rest of the way on its own, I turned to wave a "thank you" to my neighbor for his help. To my complete surprise, no one was there! Completely puzzled and with no way to explain why my pickup was suddenly able to continue up the hill (other than that my neighbor had pushed me), I quickly stopped my truck, opened the door and stood on the running board to get a better view of the road back down the hill.

Perhaps he's backing away down the hill now that he's helped me reach the top, I thought to myself. However, my neighbor was nowhere in sight. I walked back part-way down the hill to inspect my tire tracks in the freshly fallen snow. There was only one set of tracks — my own! As I drove on to my father's ranch I wondered what mission God had in mind for me to fulfill that day or what turn of events might transpire which would affect my own or someone else's destiny.

"I sure didn't expect to see you here today," my father commented as he met me at his yard gate on his way to the barn. I was too timid to tell him what had happened and figured he would think I had lost my mind if I shared with him my belief that an angel had pushed me up the hill that morning.

I meekly replied, "I didn't suppose I would make it either;" and said nothing more about it.

I spent the rest of the day wide-eyed and expectant like a six-year-old anticipating his surprise birthday party; but as far as I could tell nothing significant or life-changing happened at all. Perhaps all God had in mind was a gentle "pat on the back" since I had been spending so much time in His Word.

* * * *

Sale time was always an exciting time for me as a rancher. It was a challenge to get the calves to the sale barn in good shape and you hoped and prayed that the cattle market prices would be high on the day you took them to town. A cent or two per pound less than the going rate often meant a loss of several hundred dollars to the rancher selling his calves. If they sold well and the market was high, it was a time of celebration. If this happened, I would go to the farm store and stock up on items we needed to run the ranch and I might buy a few unnecessary things too — such as a new hat, boots, or a new dress for Karen. Then I would make my annual pilgrimage to the bank with the rest of my check to pay down our debt. Hopefully my earnings would reveal that the principal on the note was less than it had been at this time last year and I was actually making a profit.

From that time until the following summer, we would live with virtually no income from the ranch. Yet during the winter, feed bills had to be paid, taxes were due, and somehow we had to keep the house warm and put food on the table. Typically, the profit from the sale of our calves would be gone by mid-March. Then I would have to go back to the banker with my hat in my hands, and ask him to loan us a few thousand dollars to get us on through "until grass", promising to pay him back in November when once again I would be selling my calves.

When March arrived that year, I could tell by my bank account that it probably wouldn't be long until I would have to face the banker again, as in previous years, asking for some extra money for operating expenses. I only had a little more than seven hundred dollars to get by on for the next three months. When June finally came and the cows were fat from eating the new spring grass, then I could sell a few "dry" cows (cows that had failed to conceive a calf) and live on the money until sale time came once again.

I picked up the mail one morning and noticed an envelope from Reader's Digest with the words, "You may already be a winner!" printed on the outside. I did not recall entering any contests, so I was naturally curious about how I could have won something when I hadn't entered anything and immediately opened the envelope. Since then, like most Americans these days, I receive these kinds of letters every so often and usually toss them aside unopened, along with my other junk mail; but this was the first time I had ever received such a letter. I was excited to read that my name had been "selected" out of millions of entrants and I was among the few in the upper echelons of the contest still eligible to win the grand prize. If I responded quickly, the letter informed me, and returned a completed certificate "specially" placed in their "special" envelope, I would remain eligible. The grand prize was one hundred dollars a month for the rest of my life.

Wow, a hundred dollars a month for the rest of my life! I thought to myself. *Wouldn't that be fun? Just think what I could do with that kind of extra money!*

At first I thought of all the things I would buy for myself and my family; but then I began thinking about God's family too. My next thoughts were about a missionary couple I had met recently who were workers at Brainard Indian School near Hot Springs, South Dakota. I was impressed with the dedication of this young couple who had totally committed themselves to the service of God. The native American students at the school were not required to pay tuition. Instead, the school's operation was financed entirely by charity. The school's budget had been trimmed to the bone which left only a meager salary for its staff. This young couple's salary was only seventy-five dollars per month. They were expecting a baby and I couldn't see how they could ever hope to pay for its delivery with such a low salary.

I also thought of our little church and its limited budget, and of other ministers and missionaries I had met. Finally I prayed, *God, if you will let me win this contest, I'll commit all of my winnings to you. I'll see to it that every penny goes into your service.*

I went to bed that night still meditating upon the contest and what I would do with a hundred dollars every month for the rest of my life. I was certain that God would practically fall all over Himself answering my prayers and settled down peacefully to sleep.

At about one o'clock in the morning, I was suddenly awakened by an inner voice. It said, *Tom, you don't need to win that contest to have the means to help out My servants. You already have seven hundred dollars in your account. If you want to give something, give it away!*

I rolled over thinking my imagination must have taken a wild turn. I knew that with my expenses as they were, it wouldn't be long before our last seven hundred dollars was gone even if I didn't give it away. How could I possibly live for the next three months without it? Besides, if the banker found out I had just given away my last seven hundred dollars, it didn't seem likely he would loan me any more for fear that I might try giving it away too.

Once again, I heard the inner voice say, d*on't worry about what you'll live on, I'll take care of you.*

My next thought was, *Maybe this is the devil talking to me! He's trying to make me do something foolish so I'll go broke and all my neighbors will be even more convinced that it was a big mistake for me to become such a dedicated Christian.*

Sill, I couldn't shake the message I had just heard from my mind and tossed and turned in my bed for the next hour or two. Finally I decided to make a deal. I prayed, *All right God, if it was really you who told me to give away my last seven hundred dollars, I'm willing to do it. But that seven hundred dollars isn't just mine alone to spend; it also belongs to Karen. It isn't right for me to give it away unless she agrees to do so too.*

Karen was lying in bed beside me still sleeping like a baby. It was obvious to me that I was the only one at this moment that God had spoken to concerning this matter. I couldn't imagine Karen going along with such a wild scheme. So I felt a little smug that I had placed the ball in God's court, so to speak, and could finally get some sleep. Before I did, however, I got out of bed, made out a check for seven hundred dollars, and left it lying on the dining room table. I wanted to prove to God and myself that I was sincere.

When Karen woke up the next morning, I shared with her the message that had come to me in the middle of the night. Because it all seemed so preposterous, I was embarrassed even to mention it to her. As I explained the details, I did so trying to be as dispassionate as I possibly could. I wanted her decision to be entirely her own; but secretly I hoped she wouldn't go along with it.

To my great surprise, she answered immediately, "I think we should do it!"

Chapter Five

God's Style

We decided to set some ground rules for our little "adventure in faith". First of all, since God promised He would take care of us, we would rely totally on Him, telling no one what we were doing. Secondly, we would do our best not to influence anyone else, even inadvertently, to supply our needs. Thirdly, we would continue living the lifestyle we'd been living. We wouldn't skip meals to conserve on food or stay home when we needed to go somewhere just to conserve gasoline. In other words, it would be our goal to keep our situation a secret from everyone, especially our own family members and friends who might wonder what was going on if they noticed an abrupt change in our actions or attitudes. Karen and I made up our minds that, come what may, we would live for the next few months trusting God completely for our provision.

We didn't win a sweepstakes contest or inherit money from a long-lost uncle, but day by day as our needs arose, somehow they were always met. Of the six years we lived on our ranch before joining up with the Secords in full-time ministry, there was only one year that I didn't approach the banker during the spring to ask for a loan to pay our bill until the arrival of summer — the year we gave all of our money away and lived totally by faith.

The first indication that God was indeed true to His word came only a few days after I had sent our check to our friends at the Indian school. I received a letter from an insurance company that my father had purchased a policy from when I was born. He made monthly payments throughout my childhood and when I reached the age of twenty-one, as stipulated in the agreement, he made his last payment. At that time, the company gave me a settlement of nearly one thousand dollars. It was my father's way of making sure I would have the means to attend college for awhile or start a business if something happened to him before I reached adulthood. I enjoyed spending the money when I was twenty-one; but several years had gone by since then.

I wonder what this is all about? I thought to myself as I opened the envelope. To my surprise, it was a check for nearly one hundred dollars. They had made a mistake when the policy matured, they explained in an adjoining letter, and only recently someone in their bookkeeping department had discovered the mistake. They asked for my indulgence and hoped I would be satisfied with the enclosed check which made up the difference. As far as satisfaction was concerned, I had been satisfied with the policy as it was and would never have noticed the mistake if they hadn't brought it to my attention. If they wanted to make amends, however, this was the perfect time to do it.

Other small amounts of unexpected income came in almost on a daily basis as I paid our bills and met our other obligations. However, one overriding concern was an odd clicking sound that had begun emanating from the engine of our car. One day I drove it to town to ask our mechanic what he thought was causing the noise.

"It sounds like a worn valve lifter to me." he speculated. "I see you have nearly 90,000 miles on this engine and that could cause the lifters to wear. If I were you, I'd get it fixed right away. You don't want a valve dropping down into the cylinder. If that happens, it'll ruin your engine."

I'll think about it," I replied, but drove away with no idea where I could scrape together enough money to have the job done.

By this time we had lived for several weeks barely finding enough money to pay our bills, but somehow always meeting every obligation on time. We had spent the loose change in the sugar bowl and the coins that had collected in the bottom of my dresser drawer.

I checked the gas gauge the following Saturday to see if we had enough fuel in the tank to get to church and back home again on Sunday. We did, but we had no money whatsoever to put in the collection plate when the offering would be taken.

Lord, I prayed, *if I don't put some money into the collection plate like I do every Sunday when we go to church, the treasurer or the pastor is likely to become suspicious and wonder why!*

If you had ten dollars, would you put it all in the plate? I sensed the Lord asking me.

No, I responded, *I would put five dollars in the plate and use the rest to buy a can of STP to add to the engine oil so I don't drop a valve.*

All right, He replied. *Then look in the secret compartment of your billfold.*

I had riffled through my billfold many times in the past few days hoping to find a little bit of loose cash or change, even looking in the special compartment, and had come up empty each time: but in obedience to God's inward directive, I looked once more. To my delight there was a crisp new ten dollar bill tucked away directly behind the flap in my billfold's secret compartment!

On the way to church the next morning, I stopped at the gas station and exchanged the ten dollar bill for two fives. Just as we were about to turn off the highway onto the narrow road that led to the church, our engine suddenly began banging and knocking and billows of blue smoke began streaming from the exhaust pipe. I stopped the car and held Karen's hand and we began to pray. As we did, the knocking quieted down, the blue smoke cleared, and the ominous clicking sound slowly faded away! Still unsure about what had happened, we drove on to church but didn't tell anyone about our miracle. When the offering plate was passed, I grinned at Karen as I placed the five dollar bill into it. The next day I bought a can of STP and added it to the engine; but in retrospect I believe I wouldn't have needed to. I never had the engine worked on or looked at. We drove the car well over 100,000 miles and the valves never clicked again. Some friends of ours bought the car from us for their daughter to use to take to college in Oklahoma. After she was done with it, they continued driving it until it had over 200,000 miles; but they never had any engine problems whatsoever. Eventually, they traded it in for a newer car.

Every day was a new adventure and lesson in God's provision as the months went by and He met every need. With the coming of spring the new green grass came up. When the cows looked fat and healthy, I gathered a few "drys" with plans to take them to the sale the following Thursday. We had almost made it, surviving miraculously from day to day; but I still had one last bill that was due and unlike the others, the money just hadn't come in. I would be able to pay it next week when I sold the cows. It seemed ironic, however, that God had met every other need — even large expenditures. Yet it appeared I would be late in making this last small payment.

"The bill is only for three dollars and seventy-three cents," I lamented as I walked out to the kitchen, venting my frustration to Karen over this one last shortage. "It doesn't seem like God's style to leave us short now, especially when every other bill had been paid right on time."

"Three dollars and seventy-three cents!" Karen exclaimed. "Didn't I tell you? Your mother gave me that exact amount just this morning. I had picked up some paint for her at the hardware store when I went to town last fall; but she had forgotten to repay me when I delivered it to her. Then, I guess we both just forgot about it. She found the receipt this morning among her paint cans and promptly paid me, apologizing for not paying me sooner."

No more loose ends — God had been true to His Word!

Chapter Six

Getting Ready to Go

The cold winter weather in February had caused the river to ice over, except for a swift narrow channel that meandered its way from bank to bank as it flowed downstream. There had been a break in the cold weather, however, causing the ice to melt and the channel to widen. Since the river was only about 100 yards from the backside of our house, I often enjoyed looking out of our bedroom window to watch intermittent chunks of ice float by.

As I was leaving the house early one morning to feed the cattle, I asked Karen to record the Lundstrum's radio program when it came on at eleven o'clock since I did not expect to get back until about noon.

Karen often greeted me when I came in from work for lunch with a big smile and a hot meal on the table. So, I was surprised when I came home at about 12:15 that day and found her sitting in her bathrobe holding our eighteen-month old baby with only a towel wrapped around her.

"What's going on?" I asked, puzzled by the strange scene.

When Karen tried to answer me, her words came out in a flood of sobs and the only words that were coherent were "Kiley", "Lundstrum's radio program", "the cats", and "the river". Eventually, Karen gained enough composure to tell me in words I could understand what had happened.

It had been such a nice day after so much bitter cold weather that she decided to bundle Kiley up in her little snowsuit and take her outside to play. She was enjoying the fresh mid-morning air as Kiley toddled after our two farm cats when she suddenly remembered that the Lundstrum's program was about to begin. Since Kiley was having so much fun playing, she left her by herself for a few moments in the yard while she went into the house to tune in the program and turn on the recorder. As she was tuning the radio dial, she distinctively heard God speak to her in her spirit, *Go immediately and find Kiley!*

She quickly turned off the radio and hurried back to the yard where she had just left Kiley, but she was nowhere to be seen.

Where could she have gone in such a short time? She wondered, fighting off a sense of panic.

Standing still, she prayed, *Lord, which direction should I go?* The two most dangerous places a toddler might wander off to would be the horse tank out at the barn or the river behind our house. Since the horse tank was empty, she determined that the river would be the most dangerous. Scanning the river bank first, looking for clues, she noticed the cats down at the river's edge. Calling for Kiley as she ran to the bank, she stopped where the ice protruded over the flowing channel and then looked down-river to see if that's where our daughter was; but Kiley was nowhere in sight.

"Kiley!" she called again frantically. Once again, Karen heard God's gentle voice from within saying, *Stand still, be quiet, and listen.*

As she did, she heard a faint gurgling sound down around the river bend. Rushing to where she thought the sound had come from, she found Kiley partially submerged in the icy water about a hundred feet downstream. The baby must have fallen into the deep water directly behind our house; but the current had carried her downstream and had washed her up next to a sandbar. The surface of the water was right at Kiley's mouth so every time she tried to cry she choked on the water. That was the gurgling sound Karen had heard.

Scooping Kiley up in her arms, Karen was overjoyed to find her still alive. However, her face was pale and her lips had a bluish tint about them. Karen rushed Kiley into the house and quickly removed her cold soggy clothes. Then she took her into the bathroom, deciding that a gentle warm shower would probably be the best way to restore the baby's body temperature. Fearful of the sound of more rushing water, Kiley grasped her mother tightly around the neck. So Karen stepped into the shower with her, clothes and all. It wasn't long until Kiley's normal color came back and she stopped shivering as the soothing spray of water warmed her.

Confident that Kiley would be all right, Karen dried her off, got out of her wet clothes, pulled on her bathrobe, and collapsed into a living room chair with Kiley's little arms clasped tightly around her neck. It was only a few moments later when I came through the door expecting to be greeted by my smiling wife and baby daughter but found them clinging to each other in the living room chair.

*   *   *   *

A few weeks later, we attended the Lundstrum crusade at Pine Ridge, South Dakota. It was there that, somewhat on a whim, I auditioned for a position with Paul Secord's ministry team. When Paul expressed his interest in my abilities, I was buoyant by the prospect that my fanciful dreams might actually have substance to them. Yet, still it all seemed so unlikely. I owned over two hundred cows by this time but had a sizable debt against them. I was using the profits from the cattle to pay off the loan for the land I had bought five years earlier. If I left the ranch to travel with the Secords, what would I do with my land and cattle? My worst fear of all was how my father would take the news if I decided to quit the ranching business. I knew he would be brokenhearted.

However, as I had hoped, when the Secords came to hold special services in our area, they invited me to play the guitar and for Karen to sing with them during their performances. It was all so perfect that we weren't surprised when they finally asked us to join their group. Still not sure what I would do about the ranch, our cattle, or my father, I boldly asked them to give us a couple months to put our affairs in order. We would plan to meet them in Virginia in January to begin this new and exciting adventure.

They went on their way to finish the rest of their tour and I went back to work, wondering what I should do next. Because I had always been so intimidated by my father, I knew I wouldn't have the courage to tell him what we were planning unless God gave me the strength to do it.

I prayed, *God, give me an opening! Make it easy for me to break the news to him.*

I found him at the corn pile scooping grain into his pickup to feed the cattle. My heart pounding, I couldn't gather enough voice even to say "Good morning," so I grabbed an extra shovel and started scooping corn, helping him fill the pickup box.

Suddenly after nearly ten minutes, my father stopped scooping and leaned against his shovel.

"Tom," he said with a frown on his face, "I don't know if you realize it or not, but you're at a crossroads. You're going to have to decide whether you want to stay in the ranching business, or go into the ministry — but you can't do both!"

I thought, *Wow! What an opening!*

Seizing the moment, I responded, "I know it, Dad.

You're right — and I've already decided. The Secords want us to move to Virginia and travel with them, and that's what I want to do too."

To my surprise, my father nodded and said, "Then go do it and get it out of your system!"

One of our neighbors confided in me a few years later that he heard my father lament shortly after I had made my decision, "I don't know where I went wrong! I never thought I'd have a son who would turn out to be a preacher. I'll give him six months, and it will probably cost him five thousand dollars, but he'll be back and when he returns maybe then he'll be ready to get down to business."

My next step was finding someone who would take care of my cows for me while I was away. I drove to town and began asking questions at the sale barn and the local café, trying to find someone I could trust who might be interested in making a deal with me. Perhaps I could get someone to winter my cattle if I promised them a share of next year's calf crop. Eventually, I persuaded a couple of my friends to take care of a few of my heifers; but I sent most of my cows to a rancher who lived about 150 miles south of us. Our contract specified that he would take care of my cows from the first of January until the next January.

As I was at my local bank one day in December, tying up loose ends, the bank president saw me at the teller window and called me into his office. Shutting the door behind him, he said, "Tom, sit down. I want to talk to you about a few things."

Motioning for me to sit, he leaned back in his overstuffed leather office chair and then went on to inquire, "I understand you're about to leave the ranch to go travel with some preaching group from Virginia?"

"Yes sir," I replied, "I am."

"Well, in my opinion, for whatever it's worth," he commented, "I think you're making a big mistake! I don't think you realize how well you've done these past few years. You bought some land, stuck to business, and paid it off. We don't see many young men your age doing things like that. From every indication, as I see it, this is a prime time to expand your business. The price we're getting for our cattle will be going up in a few months and it will keep doing so for the next few years. A lot of your neighbors are getting old and some of them want to sell out. You've proven yourself, Tom. We'd be happy to loan you the money to buy that land and in a few years, if you'll just keep at it, I think you'll be a rich man!"

The person giving this advice was one of the wealthiest men in that end of the state. He had investments in nearly every aspect of the cattle business from ranches, to feed yards, to slaughter houses. If anyone could possibly predict the next trend in the cattle market, it would be him. I knew of several people who would have willingly paid money to get his opinion about the future market prices and would have invested their total life savings on his word alone. Now he was sharing his insight with me, totally unsolicited. I had never felt more foolish in my life when I told him that I appreciated his advice and could understand his concern, but it was something I intended to do anyway. Obviously my life's motivation and his were worlds apart and he simply couldn't understand what would prompt me to take this unreasonable course of action. As I walked out of the bank that day, I wasn't entirely sure about it myself.

In retrospect, it appears if I would have followed his advice I might have been among the thousands of farmers and ranchers who, anticipating better times, borrowed large sums of money in the early seventies to expand their operations and then went bankrupt near the end of the decade when prices plummeted. Perhaps this "foolish" course of action I took wasn't so foolish after all. It turned out that I had less to lose than either I or the bank president had previously thought.

Chapter Seven

To the Promised Land

By the end of the second week in January, we had packed our things and were ready to move. I had never been to Virginia before. Getting there would involve traveling halfway across the continent. Also, I had never undertaken a move such as this. I had rented a U-Haul trailer — the biggest I could find — but soon discovered it was still much too small to hold all of our possessions. We crammed it full of everything we could get inside, discovered how inadequate it was, and then unpacked it and divided our belongings into piles. One pile contained everything most precious to us. Another pile contained things we couldn't possibly live without. A third pile contained the things we thought we really needed but might be willing to part with. Using this method, we reloaded the trailer and got most of the things into it we couldn't possibly live without. The rest of our belongings we left piled in a corner of our vacated ranch house.

Once we got on the road, we discovered that most of the weight in the trailer was at the rear, causing it to fish-tail erratically if I tried to drive more than thirty-five miles per hour. About 200 miles down the road, we unloaded the trailer and repacked it — this time, not loading it according to how valuable its contents were to us, but by how much things weighed. After it was repacked, I discovered I could drive as fast as forty miles per hour without it fish-tailing.

When we connected with the interstate in western Iowa, the wide lanes and shoulder gave me the confidence to try driving fifty miles per hour. Everything went smoothly for a few miles until Kiley, who was sitting between Karen and me, became restless and tried to stand up on the car seat, grabbing my arm. This broke my straight-as-an-arrow concentration. Inadvertently, this caused me to turn the steering wheel slightly, forcing the trailer into an extreme thrashing motion which pulled the rear end of our car from one direction to the other repeatedly. The car nearly rolled as the trailer pushed us along at a sideways angle, each consecutive push becoming more and more extreme until we finally screeched to a stop. We found ourselves sitting crossways on the highway, across both lanes. After that incident, we decided that forty miles per hour would be fast enough! We would get to our promised land eventually.

In the wide open spaces of western Nebraska where some of its Sandhill roads still remain nothing more than cattle trails, I learned to drive more by following the lay of the land than by the road signs or highway markers. The prospect of having to drive through a city as large as Chicago began to bother me as we continued our eastward trek. After we crossed into western Illinois, I decided then to bypass Chicago altogether and travel through Indianapolis, Indiana, instead.

When we had successfully navigated the beltway around Indianapolis, we continued heading southeast toward Kentucky. I hadn't bothered to plan our route by consulting a map of the United States. Instead, we simply headed in the general direction of Virginia. I knew that Virginia was somewhere out on the East Coast and figured that anything as large as an entire state should be pretty hard to miss. We plodded along piecemeal, passing out of one state and into the next, stopping at gas stations or tourist information centers to pick up state road maps each time we did, using them to navigate our way. However, when we encountered the Appalachian Mountains in Kentucky, we realized, a little too late, that our route to Virginia was much too direct for practical travel, especially since we had such a large U-Haul trailer hitched to the back of our car.

We consulted a newly acquired road map of West Virginia at Charleston and discovered that our final destination lay directly on the other side of a large mountain range. However, the map's depiction of the narrow winding roads directly across the mountains from Charleston to Virginia seemed a little ominous to us. By this time, we'd already had some experiences trying to coax our car up to the top of mountain passes and had done our best to keep from becoming a speeding juggernaut as we inched our way down the other side. Not certain whether to turn right or left at Charleston, we finally chose to go north toward Pennsylvania and cross the Appalachians by taking highway 50 through Maryland. Our little map portrayed this highway as well maintained and almost straight.

Our only traveling experiences, up to this point, had been on the wide open spaces of the American plains. Our "system" seemed to work pretty well there. We were too naïve to realize that people who hand out free road maps to strangers are under no obligation whatsoever to insure their accuracy. Out on the Great Plains, if your map failed to depict a few crooks or turns in the road, it didn't really matter. We discovered that in the Appalachian Mountains, an accurate road map is a godsend. The one we had picked up in Charleston was an absolute hypocrite! Highway 50 appeared, on the map, to bypass the mountains. We thought it was practically a straight shot right into Virginia. We expected to be there in just a few more hours. In reality, the highway snaked its way back and forth, up and down, and actually took us across the highest mountain in Maryland.

We discovered (to our pleasure) that our car's engine had more power if we put it in its lowest gear while we inched our way up the steep slopes. If we were patient, we were eventually able to make to the top of each climb. Our biggest problem was holding everything back as we rolled down the other side until reaching the next inevitable uphill grade.

The brakes on our trailer billowed puffs of hot smoke as we used them to keep our car and possessions from rolling headlong down the slopes, becoming noticeably less effective as the day wore on. Eventually, they didn't respond at all. From that point on, I had to depend entirely on our car's already overused brakes to hold us back for the rest of our journey. I discovered that cool brakes work better than hot brakes, so we stopped every so often, usually at the top of a hill, giving them time to cool off.

On one particularly long, steep, and winding descent, I applied the brakes but could tell they weren't slowing us down enough. I realized we wouldn't be able to make the next sharp turn. There was a narrow dirt road, adjacent to the turn, that disappeared into the forest. It appeared to continue in a straight line as far as I could see into the trees. I was faced with the choice of plunging straight ahead on an unknown forest trail or trying to negotiate the approaching turn while traveling twice the speed the highway signs recommended. At the last second, I decided to take my chances on the narrow forest trail. Miraculously, it was straight for quite some distance. We crossed a creek and coasted up a gentle slope where we were able to roll to a stop, then managed to turn around at a wide spot in the roadway. We pulled over and sat quietly along the side of the road, waiting for our brakes to cool, listening to the gurgle of the brook and the whisper of the winter breeze blowing though the barren branches of the trees. In this idyllic setting, we were struck by the irony that just moments ago we feared for our lives. It certainly was good to be alive.

As we slowly made our way across the mountain range, the intensity of the grade leveled off on the eastern side. Since the brakes weren't in constant use, the ones on our car began working again and we decided to keep on traveling. We finally reached our friend's home in Culpepper, Virginia, around midnight. At last, I could finally begin to live the life that had occupied my fantasies for such a long time.

We began unloading our trailer early the next morning, hauling most of our things to the basement where they would be stored for the next few weeks. Paul and Mahala had purchased a new house on the outskirts of Culpepper, but were still in the process of finalizing the details of the purchase agreement. As soon as they were allowed to do so, they would move into their new home. Then Karen and I would continue renting their old house and could enjoy having it all to ourselves.

For the time being, however, there were seven of us living there. Paul and Mahala had a baby boy — less than a year old. The three of them slept in the master bedroom. Mahala's brother, Kenneth Snyder, the other member of the group, occupied one of the other bedrooms. Karen, Kiley, and I would be staying in the other remaining bedroom.

Our accommodations in their motor home were much more constricted. We removed the built-in furniture at the front and constructed bunk beds, leaving only a narrow passageway to the back. Karen and I would each occupy a bunk on the right side of the aisle, Kenneth's bunk was the lower one on the left, and we fitted the upper bunk with a railing so it would be safe for little Kiley to sleep on. Paul, Mahala, and their baby would share the compact bedroom at the back of the motor home.

We had a particular problem with our sound equipment, though. There just wasn't enough room for all of it to fit into the storage compartments. While we were traveling, it would have to be piled upon someone's bunk — and my bunk turned out to be the one chosen. I would either sleep on the floor in the middle of the narrow aisle or else sleep in Kenneth's bunk whenever it was his turn to drive. Since we often traveled all through the night to get from place to place, I usually didn't have to sleep on the floor. I could use Kenneth's bunk when it was his turn to drive.

Although I tend to sleep better on a soft mattress, I often preferred the floor when my time to sleep directly followed Kenneth's shift. Ken was a person who perspired profusely. It was a problem he was aware of and he took showers frequently; but when he went to sleep at night, perspiration would literally run off of him and within an hour or two his bed would be soaked with sweat. When I was driving the "graveyard" shift at three or four in the morning, I usually stayed at the wheel until I was so sleepy I couldn't stand it any longer because the alternative would be to sleep lying in a puddle of Kenneth's sweat.

Our first few weeks in Virginia were a flurry of activity. Paul had purposely left our schedule open in order to give us time to adjust to becoming part of his ministry. We practiced music until the early hours of the morning and spent our days preparing for our debut as a ministry team. Along with the remodeling of the motor home, we went shopping for matching outfits, had photo sessions, prepared newspaper releases and promotional material, and planned the layout for our upcoming record album.

Paul seemed, by nature, to be a perfectionist and worried about whether or not the team would make a good first impression when we finally presented ourselves to the public. Our first appearances as a team, seemed to go very well — perhaps better than he had anticipated. Some of Paul's acquaintances, who were familiar with his former ministry, rushed forward at the close of our services, to ask, "Paul and Mahala, where did you find these people? They complement you perfectly!"

Of course, Karen and I were elated that the common consensus among Paul and Mahala's friends was that we were an effective part of something that God had put together. More important to us than public opinion, was the sense that we were exactly where God wanted us to be at that particular time.

This was illustrated further by the unusual demonstrations of the Holy Spirit that occurred during our services in the next few weeks. None of us — not even Paul, Mahala, and Ken — had ever been in a service before where the Holy Spirit manifested Himself by moving on the people like a wave of water. At the beginning of one service in particular, the audience was seated and complacent, quietly enjoying our music. Suddenly, those seated toward the back of the room were jolted by His presence and began weeping, or lifting their hands in praise, or jumping to their feet. Then, row by row, we watched as the people responded similarly. Eventually, everyone in the auditorium was visibly affected and when the "wave" finally reached the platform where we were still performing, we too felt a sudden and definite change. To me, the room felt as if someone had opened a large window and a cool, refreshing breeze had suddenly blown in upon us. This phenomenon occurred several times during the course of our ministry with varying degrees of intensity. With such an apparent anointing upon us, the messages Paul delivered usually had a dramatic impact. Sometimes entire families came forward during the invitations at the close of our services to accept Jesus as their Savior.

The recording session for our team's album was important to all of us and we were determined to do our best. Two days before our scheduled session, however, Karen caught a cold. Our tight schedule wouldn't allow a postponement of the session, so we prayed that her voice wouldn't be affected. Instead, the cold got worse and she came down with such a severe case of laryngitis that she could only whisper when she tried to speak. Twenty-four hours before the session, trying to do something that would bring her voice back, Paul asked her not to say another word until we were ready to record. Karen complied and communicated, as best she could, with hand signals and gestures. Finally, when we were at the studio and ready to begin, Paul asked her to say something. To our disappointment, her voice was still weak and barely audible. With no choice but to proceed, we began the session and recorded the songs on which Karen had only a minor part — those which put the least amount of strain on her voice. To our surprise, her singing voice was much stronger than we had expected. She could still barely speak, but her singing voice, though weak, was soft and pleasant. As each song was recorded, her voice gained in strength and power, but we still had two or three songs we had prepared that even under normal conditions taxed Karen's vocal range and abilities. Eventually, with no other choice, we had to try and record these songs. The sound we heard emanating from Karen on these final songs wasn't what we were expecting at all — her voice was clear, sweet, and even enchanting. The final recording conveyed an innocence and purity that no amount of training could have ever produced.

Chapter Eight

Life on the Road

Paul was one of those people who believed he did his best work whenever he was under pressure. Because of this, he purposely placed himself under deadlines and tight schedules that took optimum effort from all of us to fulfill. As a result, our life on the road was one of constant movement. We often traveled all day to get to our destination, arriving with just enough time to set up our equipment and get a sound check before the service began. Immediately after the close of the service, we would tear the equipment down, pack it away, and head down the road, traveling all night to make it — just in time — to our next destination.

This approach worked all right as long as everyone and everything cooperated — and as far as the ministry team was concerned, we all willingly gave him our very best. However, there was a renegade among us in the form of one of the pieces of our equipment that seemed to have a mind of its own. It was as if its ultimate design was to ensure our utter dissemination.

It had become obvious that because of our ever tightening schedule, I might never again actually be able to sleep on the bunk we had built for that very purpose. Since I really did need my bunk for sleeping, some other place had to be found to store the extra equipment. We considered building a box on the roof of the motor home, but some of our equipment was pretty heavy and we weren't sure the roof could handle so much extra weight. Besides, it would be extremely difficult getting it up there and back down again. We finally decided the best solution would be to pull a trailer behind our motor home. We weren't too happy about that option, however, because a motor home without a trailer towed behind it is so much more flexible. It would be harder to maneuver through some of the narrow streets of the eastern cities or to travel on the mountain roads of Pennsylvania or West Virginia.

Finally, one day as he was walking down an alley, Paul spotted what appeared to be a perfect solution to our problem in someone's back yard. It was a one-wheeled trailer. The box of the trailer was constructed so that it hitched in two places to the back bumper of the towing vehicle. At the back was one single wheel which carried part of the weight of the box on a "crazy wheel" spindle. The spindle allowed the wheel to rotate either backward or forward, depending on the direction the vehicle was headed. The "crazy wheel" would allow us to back up the motor home without a lot of difficult maneuvering to keep the trailer from going in the wrong direction.

Ken and I were impressed with Paul's inspiration, but Karen and Mahala expressed a few doubts.

"Are you sure that one little wheel can carry all that weight?" they asked.

"Of course!" we assured them. "Most of the weight will be carried by the back bumper of the motor home."

I was so excited by what seemed to be such a perfect solution to our problem and by the prospect of no longer having to sleep in Kenneth's bunk that I made an entry in my diary that night before I went to sleep.

"Praise the Lord!" I wrote. "God led Paul to the perfect trailer today. It's just what we need!"

We were able to purchase the trailer for what seemed to us to be a really good price, and then we went to work repainting it so it matched our motor home. After mounting the two hitches to the back bumper, we called the girls over to have a look.

"Paul, it looks like our motor home has grown a wart!" Mahala scoffed.

But Paul, Ken, and I were certain that our problems were solved.

The first 500 miles with our one-wheeled trailer passed without any problems. It was capable of carrying our equipment, but it didn't handle awkwardly like may trailers do. The two hitches on the motor home pushed it like a wheelbarrow whenever we drove in reverse. The "crazy wheel" compensated for changes in direction so it seemed like we didn't have a trailer hitched to us at all.

We started out on our longest tour thus far with plans to travel through Ohio, Indiana, and eventually to eastern Kansas. Just outside of Elkhart, Indiana, we noticed smoke emanating from the rear of the trailer. We pulled over to the side of the highway and, upon inspecting it, we discovered the smoke was coming from its single wheel. The wheel bearings had worn out. Our schedule didn't allow much time for us to find a new wheel and spindle, but somehow we did it and we made it to our destination just in the nick of time. When we repaired the trailer, we made certain that the replacement wheel was larger and the spindle was more durable. We wanted to ensure that we didn't have that problem again. A few days later, however, at what seemed to be the worst possible moment, the bracket holding the spindle broke. Then the next day — to make matters worse — one of the hitches broke loose. A few days later, to our disbelief, the other hitch broke. About a week after that, to our utter amazement, both hitches broke at the same time as Paul was backing up. This caused the broken ends of the hitches to ram into the rear of the motor home, punching large holes through it on each side. Every time something broke, we fixed it, reinforced it, and made it better than before. But no matter how much reinforcing we did, something else we hadn't planned on either burned up, fell apart, or broke off. On top of it all, nothing ever seemed to happen to the trailer unless we were running late — which we usually were — and didn't have a lot of time to spare. Somehow we always found the time to make the repairs and meet our deadlines, but not without a tremendous strain on our nerves and on our relationship with each other.

Eventually, we abandoned the trailer and went back to storing the equipment on my bunk again. I remember writing in my diary that evening something that read like this: "Praise God! We got rid of the demon-possessed trailer today! I hope I never ever see a one-wheeled trailer again!"

In January of 1973, it was still possible to buy gasoline in certain parts of the country for less than thirty cents per gallon. Later that year, President Richard Nixon forewarned the nation that we were facing an energy crisis and that fossil fuels such as gasoline were becoming scarce. The first reflection of this shortage was a sudden rise in gas prices. A few months later, filling stations began limiting the amount of fuel that was sold. The result was shorter hours of operation at the pumps, as well as long lines of people waiting while they *were* open.

The seven of us went from place to place in Paul's Dodge Travo motor home with whatever essential personal items we selected to bring along — the paraphernalia required to take care of a baby and a two-year-old — as well as a continually growing pile of electronic music equipment. The motor home's engine was grossly underpowered for such a load. It burned large amounts of oil and usually averaged only about six miles per gallon. Since the fuel tank capacity was only twenty-five gallons, we found ourselves spending quite a lot of time stopping for fuel.

Those of us doing the driving became familiar with the nuances of the gas gauge. By watching the needle closely, we could estimate — with an impressive degree of accuracy — how much fuel was still in the tank and whether or not we could make it another three or four miles to the next station before running out. We discovered that just because the needle pointed to empty, it did not necessarily mean the tank was completely dry; we probably still had another gallon or so which we could use to travel just a little further. When the needle rested on the peg and quit moving — ever so slightly — then you knew it was imperative to get to a gas pump as soon as possible!

In June, we had meetings scheduled in Florida. Early one morning, one of our friends from the church where we had been holding services, showed up with a small fishing boat on a trailer hitched to his pickup truck. He was there to take Paul, Ken, and me fishing on Lake Okeechobee.

Although Lake Okeechobee is huge, most of it is shallow. Because it is so shallow, our friend had a special fishing technique. He would get out of the boat, walk through the water (which was nearly up to his chest), and by looking into the water while wearing polarized sunglasses, he could locate spring holes on the lake's bottom. Fish usually congregated around the cool spring holes in the heat of the day, he informed us, and by casting a line around those places, one would have a good chance of catching something.

Before following him out of the boat and into the water, we asked him, "But aren't there alligators in this lake?"

"Yeah, there are." He replied casually. "But they don't

usually come out this far in the heat of the day. Don't worry about it. You'll be safe," he assured us.

Somewhat reluctantly, we got out of the boat and waded through the water looking for spring holes as he had instructed. His system worked surprisingly well and evidently the alligators weren't hungry, so we had a great time fishing in the lake for most of the day.

We weren't aware of the intensity of the hot Florida sun as it reflected off the water onto our faces until late that afternoon. All of us had been sunburned; but Paul, who had a redhead's complexion, was the most affected. When he came home, his face radiated like a cherry.

Paul was miserable most of the night suffering from the sunburn, but since the next morning was Sunday he got up early and dressed in his new white suit, preparing for the Sunday morning services. He would have looked strange with such a bright red face anyway, but in his white suit, light green shirt, and bright white bow tie, he looked especially odd. Mahala captured the essence of his appearance when she exclaimed (in her Virginia southern drawl), "Paul, you look just like a mint sundae with a cherry on top!"

As usual, we had very little time to get to our next engagement in Maryland, when our meetings in Florida were over. In order to make it as scheduled, we would have to travel all day, through the night, and into the next day.

I took the wheel from Paul at about three o'clock in the morning. He was still suffering from his sunburn and was too tired to stay awake any longer. I drove for a couple of hours and then began looking for a gas station or truck stop where we could replenish our fuel supply. Although there were several truck stops that normally would have been open along this stretch of interstate in North Carolina, all of them were closed because of the fuel shortage. I kept driving, hoping I'd find one open at the next exit. Finally, with the needle pegged on empty, I prayed that somehow we would make it to the next exit where a billboard had advertised a truck stop that was supposed to be open all night. Four or five miles from the exit, however, the engine coughed, sputtered, and died.

Rubbing sleep from his eyes, Paul emerged from the bedroom at the back of the motor home alarmed that I had stopped along the shoulder of the highway.

He asked, "What's wrong? What's happened to the motor home?"

"I'm sorry Paul," I explained, "but we're out of gas."

We were running behind schedule as it was, and because I felt responsible for causing yet another delay, I tried to reassure him by promising, "Don't worry about it, Paul. I'll go get us some gas somewhere."

Then I stepped out of the motor home and started walking down the highway.

I walked for about half a mile and came to a semi that, for some reason, was parked along the shoulder. I stepped on the running board to look inside and found a rather hefty woman slumped over the steering wheel asleep.

I tapped gently on the window to awaken her. Looking around, she rolled down the window slightly and asked, "What do you want?"

I explained that we had run out of gas and I needed a ride to the next exit where there was supposed to be an open truck stop. She turned around and discussed my situation with a man who was lying behind her in the truck's sleeper compartment, then reaching across the cab to unlock the passenger side door, she said, "Okay, get in."

She brought her truck to life and it rumbled on down the

63

highway. She let me off at the next exit and drove away. I watched as the early morning fog quickly enveloped her truck and obscured it from my sight. When I walked from the exit to the truck stop I realized that it , like all of the others, was closed for the night too. It was then I realized in my haste to rectify our situation, I had forgotten to bring my wallet, identification, or any money whatsoever with me.

I found a pay telephone and dialed "O". When the operator answered, I asked, "Could you connect me to the local police station? We've run out of gas and our motor home is parked along the interstate. We could use some help."

"I can give you the number of the police station," she replied, "and you may dial it yourself."

I explained, "Ma'am, I forgot to bring any change with me and the truck stop where I am making this call is closed. Would it be possible for you to dial that number for me?"

Hesitatingly she replied, "Well — I'm not supposed to dial the number for you — but I guess in this case it won't hurt to make an exception."

When I explained our situation to the person who answered the phone at the police station, he told me, "I know the manager of the truck stop where you're making your call. I'll call and ask him to come down there to help you."

Ten minutes later a gentleman arrived at the truck stop driving an old Ford pickup and wearing oil-spattered coveralls. He asked, "What seems to be your problem?"

Once again, I explained what we needed but then added, "I was so upset about running out of gas that I forgot to bring my wallet along. Would you mind bringing me back to the motor home? I'll gladly pay you for your trouble and for the gas once we get there."

"No problem!" he replied.

A few minutes later we arrived back at the motor home with a five-gallon can of gasoline to pour into the empty tank. Then we started the motor home and drove to the truck stop where the manager allowed us to fill our tank.

Even though it was five miles to the next exit, it had not taken me much longer than half an hour to get our motor home refueled and running again — including the trips to and from the truck stop. We drove for at least another two hours that morning before I noticed any other stations along the interstate which were open for business. It turned out that since we ran out of gas and I was able to find a station manager to help us, we gained at least an hour of traveling time that we otherwise might have spent parked at a truck stop waiting until it opened for business.

After spending six months as part of the Secord's ministry team, Karen and I began noticing the effect that our lifestyle was having on our daughter. It was hard for her to get a good night's sleep when we traveled all night since her bunk was located directly behind the driver's seat. Because of this, she was often irritable and fussy. When we held a series of services in the same community for a few days, we usually stayed as guests in the homes of church members, in the pastor's house, or in motel rooms. Our life and the relationship we had with other people was one of constant change. The only things predictable and consistent in Kiley's life were her mother and father. We noticed, as time went by, how she was becoming more and more dependent on our physical presence for comfort and assurance. She was especially nervous and unsettled whenever we were required to leave her in someone else's care.

"This lifestyle isn't good for a two-year-old," Karen commented one day. "For her sake, I think we need to make some changes."

I agreed. It was time to face the facts. My fanciful dreams about being in a full-time traveling ministry seemed to be coming to an end.

As far as our plans were concerned, we might have returned to the ranch, but I had signed year-long contracts leaving the care of my cattle in the hands of others. I wouldn't be able to bring them back home until the following January.

Not sure where to go or what to do for the next six months, I called Pastor Lloyd on the phone and explained our circumstances.

Lloyd had left the little country church at Eli, Nebraska about two years prior to this time and was now pastoring a church at O'Neill, Nebraska.

"Why don't you move to O'Neill where we are?" he suggested, "I will talk to my church board and see if I can get them to instate you as my 'Minister of Visitation' and you can work with me."

When we left Virginia, we didn't try to load all of our possessions into one large trailer as we had when we moved out. Instead, we rented a U-Haul truck and hauled our belongings back to Nebraska that way. We planned our route before we left, carefully consulting a reliable road atlas to get an overview of the entire nation and we crossed the mountains by following the interstate through Pennsylvania.

We kept in touch with the Secords for several years afterward and noted the slow but consistent progress of their ministry and its effectiveness. Their hard work appeared to be paying off and perhaps their ambitions for success would finally come. But then one day, we heard the news that the team had broken up. Kenneth, Paul and Mahala, and the rest of their staff had each gone their separate ways.

Chapter Nine

Another Beginning

My position as "Minister of Visitation" at Lloyd's church was merely a title describing the service I might be able to fulfill to the congregation. Even before we made the decision to move to O'Neill, Nebraska I was aware that the church wouldn't be able to pay a salary. We appreciated Lloyd's ministry, however, and wanted to become a part of it. As far as making a living was concerned, I temporarily found employment working for a farmer, helping him feed his pigs. The move back to Nebraska from Virginia had cost more than we had anticipated. I had bills to pay and it was the only job I could find.

About twelve miles west of O'Neill, along the Elkhorn River, a family camp was held every summer in a large wooden tabernacle. The meetings usually lasted from Sunday to Sunday and special speakers and musicians were invited to conduct the services. The speaker for the camp that summer was a popular full-time evangelist and he would be bringing a talented young married couple with him to lead the congregational singing and to share their special music. Two or three weeks before the camp was to begin, however, something came up which, it was presumed, might keep the young couple from arriving on time for the first Sunday's services. The camp director called me and asked if Karen and I would prepare some special music and lead the congregation singing if the scheduled musicians weren't able to get there on time. I told him we would prepare something beforehand if they needed us.

Except for the time we spent with the Secords, most of

our musical experience had been with county-western or rock and roll bands. In the gospel music realm, the Secord's style had always been somewhat avant garde when compared to other musicians and singers at that time. I knew our music wouldn't be anything like what the people who attended the camp were used to so I considered adapting our style to fit their particular taste. However, when we practiced, we realized we were incapable of doing so. We were who we were, and it didn't make sense to try and pretend to be something else, so we worked up some songs in our own style. If the congregation didn't like it — then so be it.

As expected, the camp musicians didn't arrive in time for the first Sunday morning service. So Karen played her portable electronic organ and we used an electronic rhythm machine to create a drum beat while I played my electric guitar and led the congregation in praise and worship. An electronic rhythm machine was state of the art technology in those days and it was a brand new experience for most in the audience to sing hymns while accompanied by an electric guitar.

The effects of that Sunday morning's service brought an end to my occupation as a pig feeder. There were dozens of pastors from all over Nebraska and a few from its surrounding states attending the service that morning. Later, several of them sought me out to invite us to their churches for a full concert or for a weekend of special services. By the end of the week, our calendar was completely filled from then until January with concerts and special meetings throughout Nebraska, Missouri, Kansas, Oklahoma, and South Dakota.

About three weeks later, we packed what we needed into our car and headed for Oklahoma where we would be holding our first two weeks of special services. We'd planned to stay with friends while we were holding our meetings, but for Kiley's sake, we hoped we could find a motor home or a camper trailer within our price range which would provide the stability that familiar living quarters would bring.

We found what we were looking for in a used car lot. It was a nineteen-foot mini-home with less than one thousand miles on the odometer. We offered the salesman what we felt we could afford — seven thousand five hundred dollars — and he accepted our offer. The individual keeping our cattle for us had recently sold the calves and had sent us six thousand dollars, our share of the profit. And since we were able to sell our car for fifteen hundred dollars, we drove away in our new mini-home without owing a cent on it.

This proved to be one of the best deals I've ever made on the purchase of a vehicle. We drove the mini-home two and a half years, put sixty-five thousand miles on it, and when we were ready to replace it, we sold it for eight thousand five hundred dollars, making a thousand dollar profit.

Although the mini-home was small, its designer had done a good job of creating storage space and we found plenty of room for our personal necessities and other items that helped make us comfortable in our little home on the road. Compared with the space allotted to us in Paul's Dodge Travco, we felt like we were living in a spacious palace! I bought a small trailer (this one with two wheels) and pulled it behind the mini-home to carry our musical equipment.

One of our biggest concerns was how our lifestyle would affect Kiley. Would having our own private quarters as we traveled be sufficient to provide the sense of security and belonging for her? Happily, in a short while, we noticed Kiley's attitude changing as she became more and more content with our miniature home and its familiarity.

The events leading up to the formation of this new, somewhat family-oriented ministry we were now engaged in had been so unexpected and so incidental that we didn't consider ourselves particularly called of God to fulfill any special mission or divine purpose. We simply enjoyed sharing gospel music, an unexpected opportunity to do so had arisen, and it was something we could do to make a living until January came and the contract on our cattle ran out. We expected to be back on the ranch — more or less taking up where we had left off — by the early part of the next year. After a month or so on the road, however, we began receiving so many invitations to share at various churches and organizations that it became evident we could probably keep right on doing what we were doing for at least another year if we wanted to. I discussed this turn of events with the man who was keeping my cattle for me, and since we both had made a profit from the calves he'd sold, we decided to renew our contract for yet another year.

When January arrived (the milestone of our first year away from the ranch), we noted how different things had turned out from what we had expected, how much we had learned, and how much we still had for which to be thankful. Already, our schedule was almost completely filled for the entire next year. We were about to record and release our first record album. And Karen and I were expecting another baby. The doctor told us the baby's due date would be the following summer, probably around the last week in July.

Chapter Ten

Milk, Eggs, and Hair Spray

The cattle market took a sudden downward plunge in the spring of 1974 as gasoline prices continued to rise steadily. Within a matter of weeks, the dollar value on the cattle I owned dropped to nearly half of what it had been just a few months before. Like many farmers and ranchers throughout rural America, I found myself in the position of owing more money on my cattle than they were actually worth. In fact, I calculated if I sold every cow I owned at the going price and gave every cent of it to the bank, I would still owe them over fourteen thousand dollars!

From the time Karen and I were first married, it had been a common practice of mine to ask the banker for extra money whenever we were short on cash. Because I always paid it back in the fall when the calves were sold, I had gained the bank's trust and had never been turned down when I asked for these short-term loans. But now that the cattle market had crashed, I knew better than to ask.

Our ministry was doing well enough to provide us with a living, but I had taxes to pay and other unexpected expenses had arisen. When summer arrived, we were barely making ends meet and simply had nothing left over. We were expecting the baby during the last week of July, but since we needed the money I scheduled concerts and special services right up until that time.

When Karen went to the doctor for a check-up in the latter part of June, he informed us: "From the size of the baby and the way it is positioned, I think we've miscalculated the time of its delivery. It wouldn't surprise me at all if it were born at any time."

"If I were you," he warned, "I wouldn't leave town until it arrives!"

Following the doctor's orders, I canceled all of the services which I had scheduled over the next several days. Then we waited expectantly.

As the days — and then weeks — went by, I canceled the other services which were previously scheduled as the time of each one drew near. Yet the doctor's predictions remained unfulfilled. The little bit of money we had set aside in anticipation of Karen's hospital expenses slowly dissipated as we spent it for our immediate needs until it was finally gone.

Because we were still waiting for the arrival of our baby and were available, the pastor of a small church in Page, Nebraska had asked me to fill her pulpit on the following Sunday. I was grateful for this opportunity because it gave me something to do, her church would probably pay me for being her substitute, and Page was close enough to O'Neill that we could make it to the hospital on time if Karen began experiencing labor pains.

On Saturday afternoon, Karen asked me to pray with her about her shopping list.

"I know we don't have any money," she lamented, "but we need milk, eggs, and hair spray."

Other than pray, there was nothing else I could do except to assure her that God knew what we needed and I believed He would provide it somehow.

"Besides," I pointed out, "the church at Page will probably pay me something for filling in for their pastor and if we can get by without these things for only twenty-four hours more, we may be able to buy what we need then."

The day was especially hot and humid and Karen, in her

condition, was having a difficult time dealing with it. Because the air conditioner on the roof of our mini– home usually kept our small living quarters cooler than our house, we decided to drive over to the church at Page, plug the mini-home into an electrical outlet there, and spend the rest of the day enjoying its comfort.

The pastor's husband greeted us when we arrived, and after we had parked and hooked up to electricity, he asked, "By the way, could you use some milk and eggs? One of our members brought us some a little while ago, and since Dorothy and I are about to leave for the rest of the weekend, we really don't need them."

We assured him that we'd be grateful for the milk and eggs. After he delivered them, I thought to myself, *Okay, we've got our milk and eggs, now what about the hair spray? Did he forget to mention the hair spray — or will someone else bring it by later on?*

But no one arrived that evening with hair spray.

When we were getting ready for church the next morning, I complemented Karen on how nice she looked.

"Thank you," she replied. Then she added, "I wish I had some hair-spray. I don't think my hair will stay nice very long without it."

An empty hair-spray can was lying in the waste basket where it had been tossed after it was used up several days before. She retrieved the can and shook it wistfully just to be sure it was actually empty; but the can felt lightweight — as an empty can would — and there was no sound of liquid sloshing inside. Before tossing it back into the trash, however, she pushed on the nozzle. To our surprise, hair spray came streaming out. Taking advantage of it while it lasted, she gave her hairdo a quick going over. Satisfied, she set the can on the counter and said, "Well, how about that!"

Curious to see what would happen, I picked up the can and pushed on the nozzle also. As before, spray came rushing out. Since it was there, I gave my freshly combed hair a shot too. When we went to church that morning, I felt we both had especially fine-looking hair.

That evening as we were getting ready to go back to church, Karen touched up her hair and checked once again to see if the can would still spray. Like Elijah's cruse of oil, the can seemed to replenish itself. Whenever we needed hairspray, the empty can supplied all we needed.

As I anticipated, the church gave us a small remuneration for supplying their pulpit while the pastor was away. It was enough to buy a fresh can of hair spray plus a few other items we needed. Before we went to the grocery story, however, Karen once again used the seemingly empty can to spray her freshly styled hair. After we returned with a fresh can, however, our empty can finally remained empty. It wouldn't produce even the slightest amount of spray no matter how hard we shook the can or pressed the nozzle.

This incident seemed to mark our lowest point, as far as our financial situation was concerned, while we were awaiting the birth of our baby. Other churches in O'Neill and the surrounding area began asking us to share our music and message with their congregations and some of them gave us rather generous donations.

There was a Free Methodist Church camp that I had scheduled for the third week in July in a town which was nearly a three-hour drive from O'Neill. I had called the camp director in June to let him know about our doctor's warning — that we shouldn't travel anymore until our baby arrived — and advised him to find someone else to take our place. He responded by saying, "No, I'm not going to do it. I prayed about this before I called you in the first place, God told me we should have you come, and I believe we should stand by His directive."

The time went by without the arrival of our baby, yet the director stood by his conviction. Finally, the day before the camp was to begin, we went back to our doctor and told him what the camp director had told us. Our doctor, who was a committed Christian, shrugged his shoulders and resignedly replied, "The man obviously knows what he is talking about. I seem to have miscalculated the due date. The way the baby was developing three weeks ago, I was certain it would have been born by now. Since then things have slowed down considerably. As far as the way things are looking now, I see no reason why you can't go."

We spent the week ministering at the camp and arrived back at O'Neill in fine shape, still waiting for our baby to be born.

A week later, on the twenty-ninth of July, she finally arrived. She was a beautiful girl with unusually long black hair. We named her Laura Ann. Unlike the birth of our first daughter, the delivery was relatively easy.

We had been able to accumulate enough money for the earnings taken for us at the camp and from the other special services we held just prior to our baby's birth, that when Karen and Laura Ann were released from the hospital, I was able to pay the entire bill in full.

Chapter Eleven

The Lessons of Lust

The summer Laura Ann was born was the summer I had an illicit love affair and that fall was when we experienced the agony of a broken home. I'm not referring to adultery, however, nor to the breakup of our marriage. My love affair wasn't with a human being, but with a twenty-seven-foot Winnebago Chieftain motor home.

In I John 2:16, the Bible refers to the lust of the flesh, the lust of the eyes, and the pride of life. My particular temptation with the motor home seems to fit the category of "the lust of the eyes".

At the beginning of our ministry, my little family had been perfectly content with our nineteen-foot mini-home. It was a snug, secure, and an extremely compact place of our very own where we could relax at the end of a busy day. As Karen's pregnancy progressed and as we anticipated the arrival of our baby, however, I developed a longing for something with a little more elbow room.

Our bed, for example, was situated in a berth directly above the cab of the van and it allowed us less than two feet of maneuvering space between the mattress and the ceiling. The thin mattress that came with the mini-home was a little too hard to suit us, so we replaced it with a softer, thicker mattress, making a more comfortable bed but leaving us with even less room, probably only about eighteen inches. Neither of us are claustrophobic and we didn't mind the tight quarters, but as Karen's girth grew during the progression of her pregnancy, our maneuvering space diminished accordingly. Eventually, it became impossible for me to climb over the top of her if I was on the inside of the bed and wanted out during the night. If she choose to sleep on the inside and wanted to get out, I would have to climb completely out of our bed in order to let her by. Because she was pregnant, she usually wanted out to use the bathroom at least two or three times every night.

Even though I knew we couldn't afford to trade motor homes at the time, I began longing for something a little more suited to my growing family. The likelihood of our being able to do so at that moment, however, seemed very remote. We were still awaiting the arrival of our baby, we had no income from our ministry because the doctor had told us not to travel, and we had no idea how we would pay the doctor and the inevitable hospital bills when the baby finally arrived.

Then one of our friends told us about a member of their church whose spiritual gift (according to him) was "the gift of giving." He owned a Winnebago motor home and perhaps, our friend suggested, he would sell it to us for a reasonable price. With our financial status being what it was, I realized the only "reasonable price" I could afford to pay would be "free". On the other hand, I reasoned, if the man actually had the gift of giving, maybe God would talk to him about us and he would simply give it to us. As far as my logical reasoning was concerned, it all seemed pretty simple. We obviously needed a larger motor home in order to do the work we were doing and the man seemed to have exactly what we needed. I concluded that it might be worthwhile to talk to him and see what his motor home looked like.

As I introduced myself to Mr. Posey, and told him about our ministry, I was pleased to learn that he had already heard about us. When I told him we were interested in acquiring his motor home, he seemed happy with the prospect that it might end up being used in full-time Christian service. He then took Karen and me into his backyard where it was parked to let us see it. At first glance, I wasn't very impressed. It looked sort of like a box on wheels and I was hoping for something a little more streamlined. Our view from the inside, however, gave me a new appreciation for its box-like design. The square corners allowed for extra roominess in the cupboards located along the ceiling. A full-sized bed above the driver's seat was hardly noticeable, tucked away in its storage position; but when it was pulled down for sleeping, it left at least three feet of maneuvering space between the bed and the ceiling.

Karen was impressed with the dark brown shag carpet covering the floor.

"Carpet that color would be easy to keep looking clean — I would think," she commented. "Any dirt tracked in would blend right in with the carpet."

I was impressed by the spaciousness of the shower. It appeared to be nearly the size of a normal bath tub.

The one feature that pleased both of us the most was the built-in stereo system with its eight-track cassette player.

"Wouldn't it be fun to drive down the road enjoying our favorite music on tape instead of having to listen to whatever we can find on the radio?" I suggested.

We had seen enough and I was ready to try making a deal. I asked meekly, "Mr. Posey, how much money do you want for your motor home?"

"Well," he replied, "they tell me it's worth about twenty thousand in its present condition. I paid a lot more than that when I bought it last year; but I am willing to sell it to you for only twelve thousand. How does that sound?"

Normally I would have been grateful for such a generous offer, but I knew we couldn't actually afford to pay Mr. Posy anything for his motor home. I briefly explained our current financial status, but also expressed my belief that we serve a God who hears and answers prayer. I had been so dazzled by his beautiful motor home and wanted to possess it so badly that I purposely expressed our state of affairs in my most pitiful manner, hoping to jolt Mr. Posey's famous "gift of giving" into action.

He seemed genuinely touched by my story and impressed by our dedication to God but left his offer as it was. If we could somehow come up with twelve thousand dollars, he assured us, the motor home would be ours.

I spent the next few days daydreaming about Mr. Posey's wonderful motor home, yet felt sullen because either God hadn't talked to him yet about giving it to us, or else Mr. Posey was being outright disobedient. In consideration of these things, I concluded that Mr. Posey's disobedience seemed the most likely.

A few weeks after our baby was born and we were back on the road, still traveling in our mini-home, we noticed an unpleasant odor emanating from the back of our vehicle. I pulled over to the shoulder of the highway and looked the mini-home over on the outside while Karen investigated it from the inside; but neither of us could figure out where the pungent smell was coming from. I had recently replaced our old muffler with a new one and finally decided that the odor must be coming from it. Perhaps because it was new, the hot engine exhaust was causing the coating on the new muffler to smell as it burned off. I drove on, ignored the smell, and hoped it would eventually go away.

We traveled for another half-hour, but the smell kept getting worse. Finally, as I looked through the outside mirror, I noticed smoke and fire billowing from the rear of our mini-home. I quickly pulled over, drew a bucket of water from the kitchen sink, and began dousing the fire. After we had tossed several buckets of water on it, the fire seemed to have been quenched. When I inspected the mini-home to determine what had caused the fire, I found that the tail pipe, which connected to the new muffler, had somehow gotten twisted around so that it was pointed upward directly against the wooden floor. The heat of the exhaust caused the floor to catch on fire.

Nobody had stopped to help us while our motor home was still on fire, but shortly afterward a car pulled up from behind and stopped. In the meantime, I had crawled beneath the mini-home to make sure the fire wasn't still smoldering somewhere. While I was making my inspection, I heard a man's voice ask, "Do you need some help?"

I crawled out, looked up, and was surprised to see Mr. Posey smiling at me.

"What are you doing here?" I asked.

We were more than a hundred miles from O'Neill on a road both of us rarely traveled. It seemed more than a coincidence that we should happen to meet this way. We were returning home from a meeting we had held in South Dakota and Mr. Posey had been to an annual church conference and was also returning home. This untimely meeting convinced me, more than ever, that God was dealing with Mr. Posey and he would eventually give us his motor home. I was able to repair our fire-damaged mini-home, but expected to be driving Mr. Posey's motor home, instead, before too long.

In September we traveled to Oklahoma, back to the area we had been the previous fall. Our first engagement was a concert at a county fair. After our concert we were in the process of driving to the home of our friends, Errol and Sharon Hada, where we planned to park our mini-home for the night. As I was turning the corner onto a city street, I heard the screeching of tires and felt an enormous impact. It seemed as if a giant hand had lifted the rear of our mini-home into the air about four feet, pushed it forward, and then dropped it. A car, traveling down the small-town street at a high rate of speed, had collided with us, smashing into our mini-home on its rear left-hand corner.

Surviving any automobile crash is a traumatic experience, but a crash inside a motor home is, perhaps, even more so. The cupboards broke loose from their footings and came crashing to the floor. The water lines split apart spraying the debris with water and steam.

Our first impulse after the crash was to determine the welfare of our children. Kiley seemed to be completely unharmed, but our baby had been thrown from her seat and we could hear her crying loudly through the darkness somewhere among the litter. We found her beneath the remains of a cupboard, completely covered with flour, but apparently unhurt. Sharon Hada and her daughter Jamie were also riding with us and they too, seemed to be fine. Amazingly, none of us in the mini-home, and not even the driver of the car that hit us, was hurt!

The driver was the sixteen-year-old son of a prominent local businessman. We found out later that he had been involved in another automobile accident just a few days earlier. He had hit someone else's car, but had driven away without reporting it. Subsequently, he was caught and charged with a hit-and-run. His wealthy father paid his bail but his trial date had not yet arrived. His driver's license had been revoked, but he had ignored the laws and kept driving anyway. He was extremely intoxicated when he hit us, and since none of us had seen him coming before we turned the corner, I suspect he was driving with his lights off.

We slept in the Hada's spare bedroom that night and then early the next morning transported our belongings out of our "broken home" into their living room. I made phone calls to our insurance company and then to a few motor home repair shops, getting estimates on the cost of repairing the damage. The lowest estimate was six thousand seven hundred dollars.

At about seven o'clock that evening, nearly twenty-four hours after the accident, a policeman knocked on the Hada's door and asked to talk to me.

"Mr. Cobb, I'm issuing you a citation for failure to yield," he informed me. "We believe you were partially responsible for the accident."

"Failure to yield?" I asked in astonishment. "The boy hit me at the rear of my motor home! How could I have yielded to him?"

The policeman shrugged his shoulders, almost sheepishly, and replied, "Well, that's the way it's been decided."

Still puzzled at this strange turn of events, I began to consider the situation. One of the town's most prominent citizens has a son who was already in deep trouble. He might be sent to a reform school because of his previous hit-and-run accident, and now he had been arrested for driving while intoxicated and without an operator's license. These developments were certain to make his prior case in court much more damning. If the blame for our accident could be shifted away from him, however, it might help his cause. I was a visitor from Nebraska with very little influence in that community. Considering that the boy's father was a businessman with considerable local influence, the deputy may have been coerced to issue the citation in order to maintain his status among his neighbors as their public servant.

I pled "not guilty" before the judge a few weeks later

when my citation was reviewed, and I was quickly acquitted. By that time the young man had already been to trial for his more serious hit-and-run case, however, and perhaps his involvement in my accident was minimized because the blame for it had not yet been determined.

The businessman's insurance company agreed to pay for the damages on our mini-home, plus they would pay two hundred and fifty dollars per month for me to rent another motor home until the repairs on mine had been made. I called Mr. Posey in O'Neill to ask if he would rent his Winnebago to me for that amount. He not only agreed, but would deduct the money paid for rent against the purchase price of the vehicle, if I decided to buy it.

My friend Errol drove me from Oklahoma to O'Neill, Nebraska — nearly six hundred miles — to get the Winnebago. I brought a new eight-track cassette along with me so I could listen to music when I drove Mr. Posey's motor home back to Oklahoma.

It was already dark before we arrived at O'Neill, and in order to get the Winnebago back to Oklahoma in time to maintain our ministry itinerary as I had previously scheduled it, I would have to drive all night.

At least I'll be driving in style, I thought to myself smugly.

After starting the engine, I proceeded to insert the cassette into its slot, but there was no place for it.

Mr. Posey was still in the motor home with me, explaining some of its features.

"Hey, where's the slot for the eight-track cassette tape?" I asked.

"There isn't one," he replied.

"But there was one!" I protested. "That's one of the things I remember most about your motor home when you

84

showed it to us last summer."

"I'm sorry but you are wrong." Mr. Posey flatly asserted. "There has never been an eight-track player in this motor home."

I decided there was no use arguing with him; but later when he wasn't looking, I searched underneath the dash looking for telltale screw holes which would reveal that an eight-track player had been mounted there at one time. In spite of my searching, I could find no evidence of it at all.

I have determined that lust is Satan's particular deception to the human heart. His goal is to convince people that a singular item, position, or pleasure is all that is needed to bring fulfillment and happiness. The person's mind may suggest something different, but the individual chooses to ignore his logical mind and decides to believe whatever his heart has been telling him. In that condition, a person willingly believes what is not true and sees things that do not even exist. Mr. Posey had no reason to lie to me about the existence of an eight-track player in his motor home; but I chose to consider that prospect rather than admit that what I wanted to be true wasn't actually so.

By the time I got the Winnebago back to Oklahoma, we had barely enough time to load our equipment into it and still make it to our next scheduled engagement on time. We didn't think we'd have any problem transferring what we had carried in our nineteen-foot mini-home into the larger, twenty-seven foot Winnebago. Mr. Posey's motor home had seemed so spacious to us when we inspected it the previous summer. We discovered it contained larger living spaces but fewer storage compartments than our little mini-home did.

I had driven all night getting from O'Neill to Oklahoma. I drove most of the next day on our way to our next meeting, and then parked for a few hours in a vacant church parking lot along the highway to get some much-needed sleep. We got up early the next morning to hurry on to our destination.

I had driven for only about an hour when, just as I was nearing the crest of a large hill, the engine sputtered and died, leaving us sitting in the middle of our lane. There was no response at all when I tried to restart the engine and no electricity to activate my warning lights — or any other lights for that matter.

Still skittish about the mini-home accident just two days before, I was afraid someone coming down the highway from the other direction would come over the crest of the hill and run into us. Karen, battling the same fears, gathered up Kiley and the baby and found a safe place to sit along the roadside.

In a little while, someone came along who offered to give me a ride into the next town where I could find a mechanic — or at least someone who might tow the Winnebago off the roadway.

There wasn't a professional tow truck available, but the attendant at the only gas station in this small town offered to pull our motor home to his station with his pickup truck. He had a log chain that he would hook onto our front bumper and pull us down the hill and into town — a distance of about two miles.

I helped the attendant connect his tow chain to the bumper of the Winnebago and then we all climbed back inside and I steered as the truck slowly pulled us over the top of the hill. Without its engine running, the motor home's power steering was inoperable, so it took a lot of strength for me to turn the steering wheel.

The other side of the hill was long and steep and it bottomed out just before the highway entered town. As the motor home began rolling faster and faster down the hill, I applied the brakes but they didn't work. Like the power steering, they wouldn't engage unless the engine was running. Without any way to slow it down and finding it difficult to steer, we had no choice but to ride on down the hill and hope for the best.

Since I couldn't slow down, we overtook the truck that was towing us and bumped it so hard that the driver nearly lost control. We realized that since we were still connected to him by his log chain, if he lost control and his truck slid off the roadway our motor home would probably follow suit.

He got things straightened out just before we rammed him again. We were both traveling faster by this time, picking up momentum as we rolled down the hill. Because of our higher rate of speed, it was even more difficult for him to regain control than the first time when we hit him. The driver realized the only chance either of us had of making it down the hill was for him to stay out of our way, not allowing us to ram him again. However, if he drove too fast, it tugged on the chain still linking us, causing the Winnebago to travel even faster. If he slowed down too much, we would ram him again.

Eventually, as we synchronized our movements, we coasted to the bottom of the hill and rolled to a stop at the outskirts of town. Karen, who had been silent all the while, grabbed our baby with one hand and Kiley with the other. As she bounded out the door, she yelled over her shoulder, "This is as far as I'm going! Whatever this town is, I'm buying a house right here and I'm never going to leave it for the rest of my life!"

Considering what we'd been through over the past few days, I couldn't blame her.

The mechanic at the gas station was able to determine that an electrical short somewhere in the motor home's wiring was depleting the current it needed in order to keep it running. The large motor home battery had kept the engine running in spite of the electrical problem, but when its power was drained there was nothing left to cause the spark plugs to fire. This was why the engine suddenly died, leaving us stranded on the highway.

He attached a charger to the battery in order to restore its power; but because he had already started working on another customer's vehicle, we were informed it would be several hours before he could work on ours. Faced with this news, I found a phone booth, intending to call our contact at our next engagement and cancel the service we had scheduled for that evening.

As I was preparing to make the call, I felt an urgency that we should go on.

How can I ask Karen to go on after all we've been through? I pondered. *I don't blame her for wanting to stay right here.*

When I found Karen and started to explain how I felt, I discovered that she was feeling the same sense of urgency.

"Tom," she interrupted, "I can't explain it, but I really think we should try to go on."

Therefore, I asked the attendant to disconnect the battery charger because we had decided to travel on. He looked at me askance and asked, "What are you talking about? We haven't charged the battery enough for you to even start your engine, much less for you to drive it down the road!"

"I don't care," I replied. "We need to be going now if we're going to make it to our service tonight.

I turned the key and the engine started immediately.

The attendant protested further, "Okay. So it started! I want you to realize that you probably won't get ten miles down the road before it dies again and when it does you'll be in the same fix you were before. You won't have power-steering and you'll have absolutely no brakes!"

I drove away with his warning echoing in my ears. Beginning to doubt my wisdom, I turned to Karen as we drove down the highway and said, "Read me something out of the bible. I need something that will give me some reassurance."

She turned randomly to Psalms and began reading the first passage on the page. The verse she found was in Psalm 57: "Be merciful unto me, O God, be merciful unto me: for my soul trusteth in thee: yea, in the shadow of thy wings, will I make my refuge, until these calamities be overpast."

Karen chuckled to herself as she considered how appropriate this verse was — and then we both laughed together.

"That certainly expresses my feelings right now! We've had our share of calamities these past few days," I reflected.

The motor home continued to run for the next two hours. Just as we pulled into the parking lot of the church where the service was planned, the engine sputtered and died. Later on, under less stressful conditions, a Christian brother who was curious about the motor home's erratic behavior, found a loose wire, which was the root of the electrical problem, and fixed it for me. At least for the time being, our calamities were "overpast".

That was the end of my love affair with Mr. Posey's Winnebago. It, like everything material, had its limitations. Like the eight-track cassette player which actually wasn't there, many of the motor home's other desirable features I had lusted after turned out to be mere illusions also. The dark brown carpet kept the dark stains hidden but revealed the lighter colored ones to a greater degree — and even hidden dirt needs to be vacuumed up every so often. The bath tub appeared to be large, but in reality it was quite small. Whenever I folded myself up in it to take a bath my knees nearly touched my chin. Worse, I tended to get soap up my nose when I tried to wash my feet. The Winnebago's aerodynamics caused it to get poor gas mileage, only five or six miles to the gallon. Our little mini-home, by comparison, usually got ten or eleven.

Four months after the accident, the repairs on our mini-home were complete. Much of it had been refurbished thus giving it the appearance of a brand-new motor home. In such excellent condition I probably could have sold it for seven or eight thousand dollars if I had wanted. The insurance company paid me one thousand dollars to apply toward the rent of the Winnebago which Mr. Posey was willing to deduct from the purchase price. If I had so chosen, I might have become the owner of Mr. Posey's motor home and would have owed him only three or four thousand dollars. After careful consideration, however, I chose not to purchase it. Our mini-home was maneuverable, economical, and easy to maintain. We drove it for another year before we finally traded it in for a different, less box-like, Winnebago motor home.

Chapter Twelve

Our Double Life

When January of 1975 arrived, my partner in the cattle business told me he had lost money when he sold our calves in the fall and no longer wanted to keep them on a share basis. Therefore, I sold some of my older cows and when spring arrived I took the rest back to our ranch in the Sandhills.

Also, we decided to move from O'Neill back to our original home along the Niobrara River. It had sat vacant for more than two years, except for a few months when my father had allowed one of his hired men to live in it. The water pipes had not been drained during the winter and the freezing temperatures had caused them to break. Most of the plumbing had to be replaced, so this and the other necessary repairs kept us busy until early May.

Our ranch house became the new base for our ministry. It was much less accessible than our house in O'Neill had been, so we found it practical to schedule longer tours, sometimes up to four or five months. Whenever we returned home, its isolation made it the perfect place for us to rejuvenate, both spiritually and physically.

My father, who had been extremely disappointed when we decided to travel with the Secords, was pleased to have us back. He offered to watch my cattle when we were away on tour in exchange for the extra pasture grass I now had available since my herd wasn't so large and I didn't need it.

For the next few years, the course of our lives which had previously seemed so erratic, became much more consistent.

* * * *

Some of the cowboys and ranch-hands in our neighborhood seemed to have a certain disdain for preachers. Their rough and ready independence contrasted sharply to the meek and subservient attitude many people would ascribe to those God calls into His full-time service. The amalgamation of my vocations as both rancher and preacher may have puzzled a few of them — they probably couldn't decide whether I should be admired or scorned.

Branding time is a special season for many of the ranchers in the Sandhills. Certain traditions associated with branding relate directly to the old west when cattlemen rounded up their herds on the open range, sorted them to establish ownership, and then branded the newborn calves. The homesteaders put an end to the open range in Nebraska over a hundred years ago; but the custom of getting together with neighbors to round up and brand the calves is still common. The "branding" has developed into more of a process than merely searing ownership marks on the young calves with a hot iron. Usually they are vaccinated, castrated, ear marked or wattled, and sometimes dehorned — as well as branded. The process requires different individuals to perform each task, plus several ropers and "wrestlers". The calves are separated from their mothers and held in a "catch pen". The ropers ride into the pen to snare each calf with a lasso, usually by the hind legs, and with a quick dally of the rope around the saddle horn, they drag it out of the pen. Then a pair of "wrestlers" throws the calf to the ground to hold it while it is being processed. When the goal is to round up and brand four or five hundred calves in a single morning, it may require thirty or forty men who perform their respective duties.

In the late spring, after I had moved my family back from O'Neill to our ranch house, my father asked me to help with his branding. I got up early and saddled my favorite horse to help with the round up. I hadn't been on a horse for nearly two years, but this was a part of ranching I particularly enjoyed so it felt good to be back in the saddle again.

I was pleased when my father asked me to "wattle" that morning, when the calves had been sorted and we were ready to start working on them. I took it as an indication that even though he was disappointed with my choice of vocation, he still respected my abilities as a cowboy.

The "wattle" is a special way of marking cattle, in addition to the brand, that signifies ownership. We were the only ranchers within a hundred miles that used it and it often served as confirmation in our neighborhood as to whose cow it was when the brand, for some reason, had faded or was difficult to see. The ability to make a wattle was a skill passed from father to son. It involved cutting a small flap of skin on the calf's jowl which, when it healed over, formed a distinctive yet unobtrusive mark. After a few weeks, a well cut wattle grows into a protruding tuft of hair shaped like a dew drop.

Because it is hard work for a saddle horse to drag calves from the catch pen to the branding area, the ranchers usually assign this task to three or four ropers at the same time. When a cowboy has roped forty or fifty calves and his horse has pulled them all out of the pen, it is time to rest the horse. Then, at the cattle owner's request, one of the other workers gets a fresh horse and relieves one of the current ropers.

Since the calves are set free after they are processed, the pool of unbranded calves gets smaller and smaller as the morning progresses. The more docile calves are usually the easiest to catch, so when they are pulled away it becomes harder to rope those that remain. When there are only forty or fifty calves left in the pen, and there were four or five hundred at the start of the branding, these calves may be wiry and quick, taxing the skills of the very best ropers in the community. My father usually held the ropers he thought were the most talented in reserve when their special skills were most needed.

I was kept busy cutting wattles on my father's calves all morning. When there were only about thirty calves left to be processed, I was surprised when my father said to me, "I'll get your brother to do the wattling now. I'd like you to get your horse and help the men finish up roping the calves."

I was never a particularly good roper even when I was still ranching and spent a lot of time practicing. Now that I had been away from the business for more than two years, it didn't seem likely that I would have improved. *Why is he including me among the "hot-shots"?* I wondered.

A good calf roper is highly respected by his neighbors in the Sandhills and I felt honored as I rode up to the entry of the catch pen. The other ropers already there were some of the best in the community. As I went by the gate while gathering a loop on my rope, I heard one of the wrestlers comment to his partner, "Now we'll see what the preacher boy can do!"

I wasn't more than ten feet into the pen when a calf came darting by in front of me. One of the other ropers had just thrown his rope at it and missed. Seizing the moment, I made a couple of quick swings and threw my rope after it as hard as I could. The calf leaped in the air just as my loop went by and I caught him by both hind legs. Noticing the surprised look on the face of the wrestler who had made the comment about "the preacher boy", I purposely drug the calf up to him to hold for branding.

94

Lucky catch! I thought to myself as I gathered another loop and reentered the pen. *I hope I can do it again.*

In just a few seconds, the scenario repeated itself. As a calf came flitting by, I made a quick toss and snared him as well, also by both hind legs. I noticed one of the other ropers, who had just missed his catch, staring at me, looking a little bit puzzled. I pulled this calf out and then went back into the pen again, hoping for more of the same good fortune.

Subsequently, I roped five more calves without missing a loop. Then, as I was pulling still another calf to the branding area, my brother winked at me and, with a grin on his face, suggested, "You've been practicing, haven't you?"

"No," I admitted. "I haven't. I just seem to be having a hot streak today."

Eventually, I missed a loop or two but I continued having at least as much success as the best roper in the pen. Finally, there was only one calf left to be caught.

Limber and wiry, the last calf had eluded numerous attempts to catch him. Cattle are social creatures and often become disconcerted when they find themselves separated from the rest of the herd. This particular calf, now all alone and probably sensing what was about to happen to him, was in a panic. There was a slight depression in the soil along one corner of the pen where the woven-wire fence left about a three-inch gap. In desperation, the calf pushed his nose into the gap and began wriggling its way underneath the wires.

"Uh oh!" someone yelled. "Here's one that's going to get away!"

I galloped my horse over to the fence, but it appeared I was too late as the calf pushed his way through the hole, jumped to its feet on the other side, and began bounding away. On an impulse, I tossed my rope after him anyway, in spite of the fact that he was now on the wrong side of the fence and my chances of catching him were almost nonexistent. I could hardly believe my eyes when my loop hit the ground directly beneath the wire, ricocheted upward on the other side of the fence, and neatly slipped over the calf's rear foot just as it ran by.

I sat there for a moment staring in disbelief at the calf caught at the end of my rope. Then I heard someone express his astonishment, "Did you see that? Tom caught a calf from the wrong side of the fence!"

As one of the cowboys sauntered up for a closer look, he stated, tongue in cheek, "So, is that how you got started in the cattle business? Catching your neighbor's unbranded calves from the wrong side of the fence?"

Then everyone guffawed when someone else replied, "Of course not! Don't you know? He's a preacher!"

I heard one final comment from one of the cowboys after the calf had been branded and I was coiling my rope to put it away. "He sure doesn't rope like a preacher!"

*   *   *   *

We held on to our small herd of cattle for several more years. Often, when we came home after a long tour, I frantically shifted lifestyles from evangelist to rancher. In the springtime I went to work immediately, separating my cattle from my father's herd where they had been wintered. Then I branded my calves, repaired the fences, and made sure the cows had enough grass to eat and water to drink through the summer and fall. Before starting our winter tours, I returned my cattle to my father's pasture where they lost their distinction among his much larger herd.

96

Chapter Thirteen

Hard Times

I had never been to the "boot heel" (southeastern area) of Missouri during the winter before; but since someone told me that cotton was one of the crops grown there, I associated the area with the South. In my imagination, I pictured it as a place where magnolia trees blossomed and honeybees buzzed about gathering nectar.

My preconceived ideas were shattered when we arrived at our destination just south of Cape Girardeau and found the ground covered with nearly a foot of freshly fallen snow. The pastor met us at the church, as had been prearranged, but informed us the service planned for that evening had been canceled because there was too much snow. We'd spent January and February the previous year in North and South Dakota. I couldn't help but notice the difference in attitude between the people who lived here and those who lived in North Dakota. We'd conducted services in the middle of blizzards, yet people came anyway — plowing their way through the snowdrifts in four-wheel-drive vehicles, on snow-mobiles, and even on foot.

Pastor Stevens suggested we park our motor home in a driveway nearby and wait until the weather cleared up. He assured us that this kind of weather was unusual and it would probably clear up within a day or two. When it did, we would conduct the remaining services we had scheduled at his church.

The driveway sloped downward toward the street. Finding a level place to park our motor home was a common problem, so I carried wooden blocks of various sizes along with us which I used to prop in front of the wheels, or to park upon in situations such as this. I piled some blocks in front of the rear wheels, intending to pull forward and stop when the blocks were directly beneath the tires. The pastor stood beside the motor home next to the driveway so he could let me know when the tires had reached their apex on top of the blocks.

Hidden beneath the snow, a layer of ice a half-inch thick had accumulated before the snowfall. I hadn't noticed it when I laid down the blocks. When I put the motor home in gear and the tires began inching their way to the top of my makeshift ramp, one of the blocks suddenly shot out to the side, catapulted by the torque of the wheels and the weight of the motor home. As it careened along the snow, it struck Pastor Stevens directly in the shin with a loud "thwack". As he fell backwards into the snow, Karen, who had been watching from the passenger's seat, exclaimed, "Oh, it hit him!" Then she rushed out the door to see if he was all right.

I misunderstood her statement, thinking she said, "Oh, *you* hit him!" and interpreted it to mean that Pastor Stevens had been run over. As soon as I could, I turned off the engine and hurried out the door — hoping and praying he was still all right.

I was greatly relieved to find him lying on his back in the snow several feet from the motor home and not beneath its wheels. However, the concerned look on Karen's face revealed that something was wrong.

"His leg is broken!" She exclaimed. "A block of wood flew out from the motor home and hit him directly in the leg!"

Karen brought some pillows and blankets from the motor home for Pastor Stevens to lie on while I went off to find a phone and call an ambulance. Even though I was given assurance from the operator that help would be on the way immediately, my call was overlooked. The icy conditions had overloaded the emergency crews in the area, keeping them busy elsewhere. Pastor Stevens was shivering from the cold and, perhaps, from shock, so after waiting for more than an hour for the ambulance to arrive, we decided we'd ought to do something ourselves.

"I think if you helped me, I could make it to my car," Pastor Stevens suggested.

With Karen's assistance, I helped him into his car, placing him in the back seat. Considering his condition, I decided it would be best if I drove him on to the hospital myself, using his car, rather than wait for the ambulance to arrive.

The hospital was about ten miles away, but the highways were glazed with ice, making them slippery and dangerous. Familiar with the ice-covered roadways of Montana and North Dakota, I cautiously drove along at about thirty miles per hour, as fast as I dared go considering the instability of the icy highway. Verification of my prudence came every so often as we passed cars that had slid off the road into the ditch. A few of them had passed us just moments before. Yet, every so often, motorists darted around us traveling nearly twice our speed.

Eventually we arrived at the hospital and I was able to leave Pastor Stevens in the care of his doctor. I carefully negotiated my way back home through the ice and the snow which had started falling again.

The wind began blowing in the night and we awakened the next morning to the worst blizzard to hit southeastern Missouri in decades. The storm had caused the deaths of five or six people — individuals stranded in their cars because of the ice and snow that had frozen to death during the night.

A few days before the incident with Pastor Stevens and his broken leg, we were puzzled by an outbreak of small blisters on Kiley's neck and back. We'd taken her to a pediatrician to get his opinion, but he didn't act too concerned about them. He suggested that perhaps she was having a reaction to poison ivy. Although it was winter, he told us, sometimes people are exposed to poison ivy by picking up fire wood or by touching vines growing on trees.

Later that week, during the snowstorm, Kiley started to run a fever. Then when Laura, our two year old began acting sick too, we began to worry. When she woke up the next morning, Laura's body was covered with pox marks. Finally, we'd determined what was wrong with her — she had the chicken pox. Although Kiley had already had chicken pox, another doctor diagnosed her problem as being related to them. She had a case of the shingles. Shingles, he told us, proceeds from the same virus. Anyone who has already had the chicken pox is susceptible to shingles. However, it was very rare for someone as young as Kiley to have them.

During our entire winter and spring that year, we seemed to be faced with one problem after another. First the unusually long and stormy winter, then Pastor Steven's broken leg, next the full-scale blizzard, then our bout with the chicken pox and shingles.

Shortly after our children were recovered from their viruses, and as we were traveling to another meeting, I noticed the gears on the automatic transmission of our motor home were slipping. Shifting into high gear was especially difficult. One day, as I attempted to plow through a snow drift, something snapped and the motor home's high gear and its reverse were completely gone. We limped on to our destination in northwestern Missouri, rolling along in low gear at about twenty-five miles per hour.

Our motor home was only about a year old. We'd traded our nineteen-foot mini-home for a new twenty-nine foot, streamlined Winnebago — this one with an actual tape player and full-sized shower. Its transmission shouldn't have been giving us trouble, since the motor home wasn't all that old.

We had a service scheduled in Princeton, Missouri on Sunday and then we were supposed to be at a church in Nebraska, about three hundred miles away, by the following Tuesday.

A mechanic in Princeton told me the transmission would have to be replaced and it would take him several days to complete the repairs. It seemed we had no choice but to leave our motor home at his repair shop and check in at a nearby motel until the work was done. The motel was within walking distance from the church, so we were able to hold the services we had scheduled on Sunday, in spite of our lack of transportation.

I worried about how we would meet our upcoming expenses. We were facing the cost of a new transmission, plus the price of our motel room, and it would be an extra expense for us to eat at restaurants until the repairs were completed. Because our upcoming services in Nebraska were postponed, it appeared I would have to bear all these expenses at a time when the money we could have received from those meetings was needed most.

God's answer to our problems were unexpectedly met by the thoughtful, "salt of the earth", citizens of Princeton, Missouri. The pastor of the Methodist Church, where we held the services on Sunday, had friends in the area who also were pastors. He called them one by one, setting up "spur of the moment" services for us. Also, he loaned us his brand-new pickup truck for transportation. We shared at the Princeton Baptist church that evening, at an Assembly of God church the next evening, at another Methodist church twenty miles away on Tuesday, and at a different Baptist church on Wednesday.

The offerings taken at these impromptu services were exactly enough to pay for the repairs on our motor home. When I was ready to check out of our motel, I was surprised to learn from the desk clerk that different individuals from the community had taken it upon themselves to stop at his counter at random intervals and, one by one, they had paid for our entire length of stay.

With our motor home up and running again, we finally arrived at our next destination on Friday afternoon. A large snowdrift blocked our access to the parking lot at the church, so we parked along the street where a snowplow had previously cleared the snow away. After that evening's service, we had put our children to bed and were about to retire ourselves, when some teens drove by in a car and threw a rock at our motor home window, striking it with such force that it shattered. Then every fifteen minutes or so, they would race by again, shouting obscenities at us while they passed.

Our little girls were terrified and their fears were rekindled every time the car roared by again. Eventually, the teens quit harassing us. I replaced the broken window with a piece of cardboard, then I spent the next hour or so reassuring my girls that I wouldn't let anyone harm them and they should try to go back to sleep.

"What's happening to us?" I asked Karen when the girls had finally fallen asleep. "We've had our moments of adversity before, but not with the consistency we've been faced with these past few months!"

When we first started traveling full-time, I didn't have the slightest doubt that in and through everything, God would take care of us. Now, however, I could sense that my faith in Him was beginning to waver. When we were new believers, we often saw immediate answers to our prayers. Now, I wasn't sure what I should pray about. And when I did, I had no confidence that God would even answer.

I had read recently, in Proverbs 13:15, that the way of the transgressor is hard.

"Are we transgressing somewhere," I asked, "and don't even know it? We've sure had to endure a lot of hard things lately."

In our ensuing discussion, we concluded that our problem wasn't enduring adversities, it was our growing doubt that God would bring us through them. Because of our constant contact with religious people, a subtle philosophy concerning the character of God and "His mysterious ways" had slowly been ingrained into our consciousness. These ideas contradicted our original child-like faith so much so that it left us with the feeling we had nothing to stand upon for a foundation.

We'd been told that God purposely uses pain and adversity to test our obedience or to build our character, and we'd accepted these ideas as logical and viable. However, the implementation of this philosophy left us without much to pray about. If God commissions tests and trials to make us strong or to build patience within us, it seemed illogical to ask Him to remove them — or even to help us endure them. Otherwise, such a prayer might thwart the intentions of an all-wise and all-knowing God. Besides, how could I know if what I was asking was actually a legitimate petition or simply something I wanted because of my own selfish desires.

It seemed to us that Christianity was a lot more fun and rewarding when we still believed that all God wanted from us was our simple acceptance of His love, and for no other reason than that He loved us. I was beginning to find it hard to trust a God in whose character I didn't understand.

To resolve our dilemma, we decided to discard every philosophical idea we'd pick up along the way and start all over again. Since the Bible, in I John 4:16 tells us that "God is love", and I Corinthians 13 tells us what to expect from God's kind of love, we determined to accept this description as being, in fact, synonymous with the heart and character of God. When we purposely replaced the word "love" with the word "God", it gave us the following understanding: *God is patient, God is kind. He does not envy, He does not boast, He is not proud. He is not rude, He is not self-seeking, He is not easily angered, He keeps no record of wrongs, God does not delight in evil but rejoices with the truth. God always protects, always trusts, always hopes, always perseveres. God never fails.* (based upon I Corinthians 13:4-8).

Chapter Fourteen

We Need a Tire

We had driven our new Winnebago motor home over fifty thousand miles. The engine was still running well and our new transmission seemed to be working fine. Our itinerary that winter included stops in Arizona and New Mexico. We hoped we could finally enjoy the balmy weather in the sunny Southwest that we had previously anticipated in southeastern Missouri the year before. The trip would involve long distances and some mountain traveling so I wanted to make sure everything was in good shape before we started the tour.

We were still driving on the motor home's original tires which were beginning to wear pretty thin. I stopped in Valentine, Nebraska to renew the motor home's license. I also stopped by to see my friend, Denny Dolittle, who ran a tire shop, and have him replace the tires.

Denny frowned as he inspected them, writing their specifications down on a note pad.

"800 R by 19.5," he stated, "That's a size I've never heard of before. I'm sure I don't have any tires that size in stock, but let me check in my tire supplier's book. Perhaps I can order some for you."

As he leafed through the pages of a large notebook on the counter near his office, he commented, "I don't understand it. There aren't any tires listed in that size at all! I'll have to call my supplier. Give me an hour or two. When I find out where I can get this kind of tire, I'll call and let you know."

Since I planned to come through Valentine again before we started our tour, I could have the tires mounted at that time. So, I drove home.

I was surprised when Denny didn't call me later that day. It was two days later when I finally received my expected call.

"Tom," Denny reported, "I've called just about every major city in this end of the country, trying to find your motor home tires without much success. I was beginning to wonder if there was anybody anywhere who sold them. I know you told me you need six tires, but I could only locate two of them. And that's from a supplier in Oklahoma. I can have them shipped up here in a couple of days, but your cost will be two hundred and twenty dollars per tire, plus shipping. Do you still want them?"

Since the existing tires were wearing so thin and I didn't know what else to do, I agreed to pay the shipping charges and ordered the new tires. When they arrived at Valentine, I had Denny mount the new tires on the front, put the best of the four old ones on the back, and had him keep one of the bald ragged tires to use as a spare. I expected to find more new tires somewhere else while we were on tour — perhaps in Denver or Phoenix.

One of our first stops in Arizona was at Globe, a mining town in the mountains about seventy-five miles northeast of Phoenix. To our surprise, there was about four inches of fresh snow on the ground when we arrived. Our friends living there told us that because of the higher elevation, it snowed there once in awhile; but it would probably melt away within a day or two. As it turned out, we held services in that area for the next two and a half weeks and the ground remained covered with snow during most of that time. My hope that we may be able to spend a winter somewhere far enough south so that we wouldn't be affected by the cold and snow remained unfulfilled. We drove into warmer temperatures, however, when we moved on to Phoenix where we had a weekend scheduled. Then we had one more stop in Arizona, at Tucson, before our schedule required us to travel on to New Mexico. After that we'd be going north again through Colorado and into Wyoming.

Driving down the highway on our way to New Mexico — near Wilcox, Arizona — I noticed the motor home didn't seem to be handling properly. When I stopped to inspect the tires, I discovered that one of the rear tires, an inside dual, was flat. Since it was only about a mile to the Wilcox exit off of the interstate, and the remaining tire would carry us that far, I drove on hoping to find a tire repair shop.

Driving down the exit ramp, I noticed two truck stops, one on each side of the highway. I started to pull into the nearest one, but I sensed the Lord speaking to me saying, *don't go to that truck stop. Go to the other one instead — the one on the other side of the highway.*

I complied, but found it difficult to enter that particular truck stop. There was new construction taking place there and piles of asphalt left only a narrow lane which offered access to the services bays. After we were parked, I learned that this truck stop was being torn down to be replaced with a shopping center.

I found a service attendant who removed the flat tire, and once he did, he showed me a long ragged gash in the sidewall.

"Is there anything you can do to make it hold air?" I asked hopefully.

"No Sir!" the attendant replied. "It will have to be replaced."

"Can you get me a new one?" I asked.

As Denny had done, he looked through his order book but found nothing listed.

"You might find one in Phoenix," he suggested.

I told him I had already tried to find one there and had failed.

"Then your next bet would be to go on to Albuquerque, New Mexico, I suppose," he offered. "Albuquerque is about two hundred and fifty miles on down the road."

Considering the shape the other tires were in, I had serious doubts that we would make it that far. Although my spare tire still held air, it wasn't in much better shape than the tire with the gash in it.

While the service attendant and I were discussing my options, I noticed one of the construction workers park his tractor, turn off the engine, and walk toward us.

As he approached, he smiled broadly and asked, "You need a tire, don't you?"

"Yes I do," I answered, "but I have a problem. It seems that tires in this particular size are nearly impossible to find."

"Well'', its an interesting thing," he countered, "I found a tire lying in the ditch along the interstate the other day, and, since there didn't seem to be anything wrong with it, I took it home with me. It's a size I hadn't seen before but it looks a lot like this tall skinny tire of yours with the big hole in it. If you want me to, I'd be willing to go get it and then we'll see if it's really what you need."

"Well, that's up to you," I answered, "But if I could somehow find a tire to replace this one, I'd be very grateful."

As he climbed into his pickup and drove away, I expressed my negative thoughts to Karen, "Well, good luck, I'd say the chances that he actually found the tire we need lying along the interstate are about one in a million."

He was gone for nearly half an hour. Another man was with him when he returned. The two of them got out of his pickup and after he had lowered the tailgate, he pulled what appeared to be a brand new tire from the box and stood it on edge for me to inspect. It was a duplicate of the tires that Denny had located for me from Oklahoma. Tires I had willingly paid more than two hundred and twenty dollars apiece for and felt fortunate to acquire, even at such a high price.

Trying to contain my excitement because I knew the stranger had me at a disadvantage, I timidly asked, "How much do you want for this tire? It seems you have exactly what we need."

Considering our desperate circumstances, I may have been willing to pay an exorbitant price for the stranger's tire, but I didn't want to reveal that fact to him.

I was wearing a belt with the words, *"Jesus is Lord"* imprinted on its brass buckle. The stranger's accomplice (whom we learned later was his father) grinned as he read my buckle and said, "I'll tell you what — I think people who walk around wearing belt buckles that say *Jesus is Lord* on them ought to have all the help they can get. What would you say if we just gave this tire to you?"

I consider "free" to be a pretty good price so I responded eagerly.

With no reason to hide our excitement any longer, Karen and I openly expressed our gratitude and praised the Lord for supplying exactly what we needed in such an unusual manner.

"As far as I know," I remarked, "this is the only other tire of this particular size west of the Mississippi. And then somebody traveling down the interstate the other day happens to lose it off of his truck at just the right spot so that you would come along and find it. I just happened to have a blow-out a little way up the road from this particular exit. Then I pulled into this truck stop instead of the one across the highway. Here I was, needing a tire — and here you are with exactly what I need! What are the chances of that happening entirely by accident?"

We introduced ourselves to the two men while the service attendant mounted our new tire.

In response, the older man quipped, "I'm the only Ernest Hart you'll find here in Wilcox." then he added. "And this is my son, Philip."

As we visited, they asked us why we were traveling through Wilcox. When we told them about our work and ministry, they told us to let them know whenever we planned another tour through their area. Perhaps we could hold services in their church sometime.

We've returned to Wilcox several times since then and have held numerous services at the Hart's church. And because of their recommendations, we've held meetings at other churches throughout Arizona and California too.

How different things may have been if I had been insensitive to the Lord's leading when I felt Him telling me, *Go to the truck stop on the other side of the highway.* Without finding a replacement tire, we probably would have driven on down the road with our ragged spare tire taking us as far as it could— and who knows where that may have been? Philip Hart had exactly what we needed and he was working away on his tractor just across the highway.

After this, I called the Winnebago factory to find out why the tires on our motor home were so hard to find and to ask how I could replace them. They told me they had an abundant supply of tires which I could order directly from them. Afterward, as long as I owned the motor home, that's where I got them.

*   *   *   *

In early February we arrived at Gillette, Wyoming, where we had a weekend of services scheduled. One evening the temperature plunged to twenty-five below zero and the steady wind that blew during the night brought the chill factor down to sixty-five below, according to the local news.

Our motor home wasn't designed for such extreme conditions. We draped blankets and towels in front of the doors and windows for extra insulation and tried to stay warm as best we could. There were two small furnaces, each one placed strategically at opposite ends of the motor home; but despite their constant use, they were overpowered by the cold. A bowl of water that Kiley had placed on the floor for her pet kitten to drink from froze solid during the night.

The irony of our situation was that while everything was freezing on the inside of our motor home, the food we had stored in our refrigerator was thawing out. Even with the thermostat set at its lowest, the refrigerator was not cooling. A few days before, I had hired a refrigeration expert to look at it and he told me it couldn't be repaired. RV refrigerators, he explained, are charged with ammonia rather than with Freon (as normal refrigerators are) and if the ammonia somehow leaks away, it cannot be replaced. He advised me to discard our refrigerator and buy a new one. However, RV refrigerators are generally more expensive than those used in normal homes. According to a supply catalogue, it would cost over $1,200 to replace it. Considering the penetrating cold we were enduring at the time, it wasn't hard for us to get by without it. Karen simply removed all the things stored in the refrigerator and placed them in a box beside the motor home's door.

The rest of us were tucked away in bed for the night, snuggling under the warm blankets, but Karen was still up reading her Bible.

Suddenly, she exclaimed, "Tom, I believe if you really wanted to, you could fix my refrigerator!"

"What do you mean I could fix it?" I argued. "I've taken it to the best refrigerator repair man I could find and he said it couldn't be fixed."

"I don't care," she replied. "I know you could fix it if you would only make up your mind that you could!"

I hadn't slept very well the night before because the incessant wind had rocked our motor home back and forth all night long. Also, I was worried that the water lines would freeze during the night (they had before) and I would have to spend several hours the next morning thawing them out. Perhaps it was because of the stress of the cold temperatures, or because I wanted so badly to return to warmer Arizona, but I took offense at her statement and received it as an accusation. I angrily climbed out of bed and said, "Okay, we'll just see about that!"

I grabbed a handful of my tools and without bothering to get dressed or even put on a coat, I bounded out the door (in my pajamas) into the freezing cold. I proceeded to unlock the outside compartment door which would give me access to the refrigerator's mechanism.

When I come back from outside, shivering and cold, then she'll feel sorry for me, I thought to myself as I pouted childishly, *she doesn't appreciate all that I do for her.*

As I stared into the refrigerator compartment, I sensed a strange endowment of knowledge from God such as I had never experienced before. I didn't hear His audible voice or receive any particular message in my spirit; but I had an indomitable awareness about the workings of our refrigerator and suddenly knew what was causing it to malfunction. As if by instinct, I turned some screws and checked a few wires.

112

Using a screwdriver, I cleared some soot away that had collected on the orifice. Instantly, the sickly yellow gas flame which heated the refrigerator's coils, turned a "healthy" blue — the color it was supposed to be. Not able to explain why, I knew in my heart that the refrigerator was fixed. Yet, the entire experience had taken less than two or three minutes.

Even though I hadn't been outside long enough to even start shivering yet, there was nothing left for me to do but to go back inside. When I stepped through the motor home door, Karen grinned at me and said, "See! You fixed it, didn't you?'

When she said this, I knew she wasn't chiding me because of my previous display of childishness. Instead, I could tell by the expression on her face that she had experienced the same connection with God's Spirit that I had felt.

With a sheepish grin on my face, I answered in astonishment. "Yes I actually think I did."

"You didn't give me a chance to tell you," she explained, "when you grabbed your tools and went outside; about the revelation I had received from the Lord. A few minutes ago, while I was reading my Bible, I found a verse that says, *I can do all things through Christ which strengthens me.* (Philippians 4:13)

"I'm beginning to see that we, as believers, possess resources and talents beyond those that we were born with or even those we've developed through training. They've been promised to us in the Bible and they belong to anyone who has the faith to receive them. Our only connection to these resources is through God's Word. If we're going to operate in them, we have to stay in God's Word."

My experience with our refrigerator convinced me that

113

she had uncovered a powerful truth.

Chapter Fifteen

Heaven's Connection

We were at Rapid City, South Dakota making preparations to travel on to Prairie City, South Dakota. I had ordered new tires for our motor home from the Winnebago factory in Iowa which had been shipped to a tire shop at Rapid City. The service men were changing them for me. We continued using the trailer we had pulled behind our mini-home after we got our new motor home and loaded it down with musical instruments, amplifiers, sound equipment — things we needed to hold our meetings. The motor home's spare tire rack was located directly above the rear bumper near our trailer's hitch.

Had I realized the trailer tongue would be so much in the way as the tires were replaced, I would have disconnected it. When I removed the spare and headed toward the tire shop, I momentarily forgot about the tongue of the trailer (which was about eighteen inches from the ground and parallel to the pavement) and tripped over it. I fell sprawling to the ground, flinging the tire through the air, bruising my shins. A few minutes later, I tripped over the tongue again as I tried to take a short cut between the trailer and the back of the motor home. This brought new bruises to my shins and venom to my attitude. This just wasn't my day. I couldn't seem to avoid hitting the trailer's tongue that morning. By the time the new tires were mounted and the spare was back in place on its rack, I had stumbled over it nearly a half-dozen times.

Even though we didn't need to be in Prairie City until the next afternoon, we began the trip (which shouldn't have taken more than three hours) after lunch. We didn't have any other engagements, so we intended to arrive a day early to have extra time to get things set up there.

With Karen seated beside me in the passenger's seat, I drove and we visited amiably for awhile. Our girls entertained themselves on the couch, playing with their toys. Our friendly chat turned sour, however, when Karen asked my opinion about a hypothetical, theological issue and we discovered that my views were the opposite of hers. Before long, we found ourselves in the middle of a heated argument.

It was during this verbal debate that I felt what seemed to be a slight yank at the rear of our motor home. I was so engaged in our argument that I didn't bother to pay much attention to what was happening. Finally, glancing at the side mirror, I caught the reflection of a two-wheeled trailer in the process of passing us. For a brief moment, I paid no attention to it because my mind was having difficulty shifting from our conversation to what was happening to us, at that very moment in the real world. Suddenly, I was jerked back to reality as my mind sorted out the gravity of the situation. I processed the information something like this: *Hmm — a trailer is passing us. How unusual.* (I pause for a moment as that truth soaks in.) *Wait a minute! I think I recognize that trailer!* (Then suddenly the full impact of it all finally hits home.) *Whoa! That's our trailer! Oh no, it's loose and it's going to crash in the ditch!*

For a few seconds, it appeared as if my fears were somehow going to be allayed. The trailer stayed parallel to our motor home while its tongue slid over the asphalt, keeping pace with us. Then as it veered to the left, the tongue burrowed into the soft loose soil at the highway's shoulder, plowing a furrow deeper and deeper into the dirt. This brought the trailer to an abrupt halt — something like a horse that stops while planting all four feet, catapulting its rider from the saddle over its head. The trailer's framework stayed in place, but its upper portion broke apart, careening into the ditch with all of our equipment, through the roadside fence and into a cow pasture. I watched in horror as guitars, speakers, record albums, and even Karen's sewing machine sailed through the air in a cloud of dust.

As I pulled the motor home to a stop, I struggled against an irrational desire simply to drive away as if nothing had happened. *I don't want to face this*, I thought to myself. *I'd just like to leave and let the highway department clean up the mess.*

Since the accident had taken place along an isolated stretch of highway a few miles north of Sturgis, South Dakota, we had time to pick up the debris — the loose record albums, cassette tapes, microphones, cables, and other pieces of equipment that littered the roadway.

We soon heard the sound of a car approaching from behind the hill. The motorist realized, however, that an accident had just occurred and safely slowed to a stop. Rolling down his window, he asked if any of us had been hurt. After we assured him we were unharmed, he got out of his car and obligingly helped us finish clearing the roadway. When it appeared we didn't need any more help, he got in his car and drove away.

Nearly ten minutes passed before another car came our way. We were still busily engaged in gathering our belongings from the ditch and pasture, placing them in piles along the side of the road. Two young women, probably in their twenties, were in the car. As they stopped on the shoulder, the driver rolled down her window and asked, "Do you need some help?"

Karen started explaining what had happened and, as she

was talking, the woman interrupted her and asked. "Are you the Cobbs?"

Surprised at this, Karen answered, "Yes, we are."

"I recognize you!" the woman exclaimed. "I was at the Rainbow Bible Camp when you shared at its dedication last year." (She was referring to a service we had held north of Rapid City at a cattle ranch. The owner had converted his ranch into a Christian Bible Camp for children.)

"If you'd like," she suggested, "I'll drive to the next town, call my husband, and have him bring his flat-bed trailer. You can load the debris on it and take it to our farm. It's only about ten miles from here and you're welcome to park there until you get your trailer fixed or find a new one. In fact, my husband is handy with tools. Maybe he can help you rebuild this one."

The husband, a young man named John Williamson, arrived within the hour with a flat-bed trailer hitched to his pickup. We were able to get all of our paraphernalia, even the framework of our demolished trailer, in one load.

We arrived at this farm at about five-thirty in the afternoon. Anxious to find out just how extensive the damage was, the first thing I did was unload the musical equipment to check it out. Considering its covering of dust and the fact that some of it had landed hundreds of feet beyond the roadway in the pasture, it seemed likely most of it would be severely damaged — perhaps beyond repair.

Our most expensive piece of equipment was a portable electric grand piano. We had paid over four thousand dollars when we bought it about a year earlier. It was the first roadworthy piano Karen and I had ever heard that produced a genuine piano sound, yet it was more portable than any regular piano at that time. When its components were assembled, it became a virtual piano weighing probably two hundred pounds, complete with strings and hammers. Because of this, it required professional tuning from time to time. When I gathered our equipment at the accident site, I found that one of the piano's three main parts (the piece containing the strings) had landed beyond the fence in the cow pasture. Such an impact would be akin to tossing a Steinway piano off of a second story balcony. I remember thinking, *This is probably going to need some major repairs if we ever hope to get it working again.* Yet, after we unloaded it and assembled it, we were amazed when Karen first struck the keys. Instead of disharmony, we heard rich beautiful tones as she continued playing chords and arpeggios. Not a single string was out of tune.

Relieved that our piano appeared to be completely undamaged, my next concern was the condition of my guitar amplifier. This particular amplifier required nearly a dozen sensitive vacuum tubes to produce its sound. Once, a few months earlier, it had accidentally fallen over. It landed on its back onto soft carpet, yet I still had to replace three shattered tubes. Considering the fragile nature of its components, I wasn't sure what to expect after the impact of the trailer wreck. The first thing I noticed was a crack along the top of the amplifier's wooden frame. Directly beneath the crack was the housing where the fragile tubes were located. Once again, however, we were surprised when not one vacuum tube was broken and my amplifier still performed as if nothing had happened to it, in spite of the apparent damage to its case.

"Wow!" I exclaimed. "This is amazing! We must have had an overtime crew of angels on the job, each of them catching this stuff as it came down."

As we tested each remaining piece of equipment, we were relieved to discover that in spite of the dust and damage all of it still worked as if nothing had happened.

While we were still marveling at the lack of damage to our equipment, we were interrupted by John Williamson's mother, who announced, "If you'd like to join us, I have supper ready and waiting for you at my house." (John, his parents, and grandparents all lived on the farm in separate houses.)

Since we hadn't been there long enough for Mrs. Williamson to have prepared an elaborate meal, I expected that she had made extra sandwiches or may have added a little more water to the soup to accommodate her newly arrived guests. The aroma filling her house as we entered the doorway changed my expectations. Surveying the dining room table, I found it loaded down with all kinds of wonderful foods such as fried chicken, fresh baked rolls, mashed potatoes and gravy, and a choice of three different kinds of pie for dessert. The table was set with fine china and shining silverware.

Suddenly ravenous, I was anxious to sit down and begin enjoying the feast but Karen, with an endowment of more grace than I have, exclaimed, "Mrs. Williamson, you've prepared this meal for company, haven't you?"

Mrs. Williamson answered, "Yes, dear. I have."

Karen continued, "We really appreciate your hospitality and good intentions but you shouldn't serve us the food you've prepared for your other guests."

It all looked and smelled so delicious that even though I knew Karen was doing the proper thing, I glared at her as she further suggested, "We have food out in our motor home that I can fix for us. You should save this food for your company."

Great! I thought to myself sarcastically. *We probably will have sandwiches and watered down soup in our motor home.*

But Mrs. Williamson simply answered. "No you are the company that I prepared all this for."

"How could you have?" Karen asked. "It's obvious you didn't prepare all of this in the last hour. You couldn't have known we were coming before then."

Mrs. Williamson explained. "When I first get up in the morning, I always spend some time reading my Bible and praying. I'd already decided not to spend much time in the kitchen today since the day had already started out so warm. I intended to serve just leftovers for supper; but the Lord spoke to me during my prayer time and told me to prepare a special meal tonight. *"You will be having company."* He told me. He wanted me to get things ready for when they arrived. I've been cooking most of the day. I thought I might be feeding extra men tonight, since it's harvest time now, but you came along instead — and right on time too!"

After we had enjoyed the wonderful meal, John, his father, and I went to their workshop and started to work, repairing the demolished trailer. I helped as John and his father welded the broken pieces back together and heated the twisted metal, binding it back in shape.

At about midnight, we stepped back to admire the reconstructed trailer. It had been completely rebuilt. It was hard to believe that less than eight hours ago the same trailer was in pieces, scattered along the highway.

The Williamsons refused to accept any money for their hard work or hospitality. We left their farm the next morning at about nine o'clock with our trailer safely hitched to the motor home and our sound equipment inside.

I was impressed by the Williamson's connection with God — particularly, Mrs. Williamson's ability to know and act upon His directives. Following her example, I began spending more time reading the Bible and praying.

A few days later, during one of these times of soul searching, I asked the Lord a question: *At almost the exact time I was busting my shins on the trailer tongue as we were mounting our new tires, you were telling Mrs. Williamson to prepare a big meal so we could enjoy it with her. Why didn't you say something to me that morning too? Obviously the hitch on the trailer was about to break and it should have been easy to see. It's not that I don't appreciate the way you picked up the pieces for us after the accident, but wouldn't it have been easier if you would have just said, "Tom, your trailer hitch is about to break?" Then once I got it welded, you could have told me, "Now, go to Mrs. Williamson's house and have supper." Why did you talk to her and not to me?*

His answer was one I wasn't expecting: *I spoke to both of you that morning. She was listening, but you weren't!*

A few days later, as I was reading my Bible, I was impacted by the message in II Timothy 2:22 - 26. It read: "Flee also youthful lusts: but follow righteousness, faith, charity, peace, with them that call on the Lord out of a pure heart. But foolish and unlearned questions avoid, knowing that they do gender strife. And the servant of the Lord must not strive; but be gentle unto all men, apt to teach, patient. In meekness instructing those that oppose themselves; if God per adventure will give them repentance to the acknowledging of the truth; And that they may recover themselves out of the snare of the devil, who are taken captive by him at his will."

Recalling the day of the trailer wreck, I remembered how I had started the day out angry and irritable. Then, as we were driving down the road, Karen had asked what I now consider a "foolish and unlearned question". I had not avoided it. Consequently, it had led to strife and argument. In that condition, Satan had effectively taken us "captive at his will". Because God is gracious and people were praying for us, He put all of the pieces back together. To avoid these kinds of circumstances altogether requires special obedience. We must continue to "walk in love" in order to stay away from strife.

I was so convicted by this Biblical injunction that I went to Karen immediately, vowing not to be in strife with her ever again. Rather, I promised I would remain in a position where, if Satan was laying a trap for me, I could hear God forewarn me. Karen understood and reciprocated with a similar pledge. Both of us, at one time or another have backslidden on this; but whenever we do, we ask for forgiveness and renew our commitment to it. It seems that Satan tests us every so often, attempting to weaken our resolve. He probably realizes just how much more powerful we are when we stand united.

Its importance was reaffirmed about a year later. As before, I awakened in the morning feeling irritable and unfriendly. Karen seemed to be having the same battle. Since it was difficult for us to be civil with each other, we stayed quiet and didn't say much at all.

Later, as we traveled down the highway, Karen opened her Bible and began reading it aloud. Even this annoyed me, but I stayed silent, realizing this was her way of combating the sullen spirit of depression that engulfed us. As she read and as I concentrated on the message the Scriptures contained, my irritable spirit slowly receded. Finally, after about an hour, I interrupted her.

"Karen, " I said, "Something's wrong. My thoughts keep going back to our trailer and I feel anxious about it. It doesn't have a spare tire. Maybe I should buy one for it."

As I was speaking, I saw a sign advertising an auto salvage yard just down the road a few hundred yards. Seeing the opportunity, I pulled into the parking lot.

"I need to measure one of the existing wheels to make sure I get a spare that fits," I explained as I searched for a ruler in my tool box.

Crouching at the trailer wheel, taking measurements, I distinctly heard the Lord speak to my spirit. *Check the tongue on your trailer!* I looked, but found nothing wrong. I had almost dismissed it as nothing more than my imagination when I heard the same directive again. *Check the tongue on your trailer!* Taking a closer look by sliding on my back beneath the axle (in the mud, no less), I inspected where the tongue was attached to the framework. Then I saw where the metal had cracked and the welds were broken apart. There was only a thin strip of metal, about a half-inch wide, still holding it in place. We probably wouldn't have traveled down the road another mile before it would have broken, leaving the trailer free to "self-destruct" all over again.

That particular day, we were traveling a busy highway in Iowa, much different than the secluded roadway in South Dakota. It is likely the outcome of a second mishap with our trailer would have been much more complicated and more serious, than the first had been. But we don't know that for sure, because it never happened.

Chapter Sixteen

A Better Resurrection

The eleventh chapter of Hebrews, I've been told, is God's "Hall of Fame" of the faithful. It speaks of people like Noah, Abraham, and Moses who overcame extreme adversities and achieved outstanding accomplishments through the application of their faith in God's promises. As I was reading this chapter one day, I noticed something that puzzled me. It said that these people *"subdued kingdoms, wrought righteousness, obtained promises, stopped the mouths of lions, quenched the violence of fire, escaped the edge of the sword, out of weakness were made strong, waxed valiant in fight, turned to flight the armies of aliens, women received their dead raised to life again."* (Hebrews 11:33 - 34) What puzzled me was what happened to some of these people as revealed in the following verse. It said: *"And others were tortured, not accepting deliverance; that they might obtain a better resurrection..."* (Hebrews 11:35)

This chapter indicates that faith is the one single factor which moves God to provide mankind's greatest needs — protection, strength, encouragement, victory, and even life itself. The people mentioned apparently knew how to use their faith to acquire whatever they needed.

If so; then why were the "others" tortured because they would "not accept deliverance." The way the sentence is phrased, it seems to indicate they knew how to use their faith to obtain deliverance from their sufferings, but deliberately chose not to in order "that they might obtain a better resurrection".

Why, I asked myself, *wouldn't they accept deliverance*

when they knew it was available and could acquire it at any time? What was this "better resurrection" they seemed so intent on achieving?

In my experiences with the use of faith, deliverance in itself seems hard enough to acquire. *If I succeed in using my faith up to the point that I am assured deliverance is mine,* I thought to myself, *I certainly can't think of any reason why I would choose to let it pass me by, simply for the sake of a better resurrection.* As far as I was concerned, any resurrection at all would be good enough.

From the time Karen and I were first married, we'd always been in debt. When we purchased our new motor home, we had taken out a loan and were making monthly payments. This began bothering me, however, because we received donations from our supporters who gave to our ministry with the intent that their support would help us spread the Gospel. Interest rates were extremely high and a sizable chunk of the money given to us went directly to the bank. Because we were accountable to meet these obligations, it limited our sense of freedom, especially when we were setting up our traveling schedule. 2 Timothy 2:4 states: *"No man that warreth entangleth himself with the affairs of this life; that he may please him who hath chosen him to be a soldier."* (2 Timothy 2:4) We felt that our obligations to the bank were sort of an "entanglement". With this as an incentive, Karen and I determined to get out of debt and then operate our ministry on a "pay-as-you-go" basis.

However, we had the same problem everyone has when trying to get out of debt. We had to pay last year's bills while still meeting this year's expenses and that isn't an easy task. We were making five hundred dollar per month payments on our motor home and we had regular expenses and other debts as well. It would require extreme discipline, wise stewardship, fierce determination, and many miracles from God to accomplish this goal.

Somehow, we'd been able to survive the summer and on into the fall paying all of our bills, making our payments, and meeting expenses. But when Thanksgiving approached, we were concerned because we hadn't yet been able to set aside any extra money to buy Christmas presents for our children.

That year, we didn't spend Thanksgiving on the road as we usually did, but came home on the previous Monday. I had a few other meetings scheduled between Thanksgiving and Christmas, beginning on the following Saturday. During this time at home, I spent a few days cutting and piling up firewood for the Christmas holidays.

Admiring my large wood pile, Karen suggested, "You know I think we have more than enough for ourselves. Why don't you haul a couple cords over and share it with the McGaugheys."

Our neighbors, the McGaugheys, were a semi-retired ranch couple. Mrs. McGaughey often shared produce from her garden with us. Karen's suggestion seemed like a good idea.

Mr. McGaughey seemed pleased to have the extra wood, so while I was unloading it he went into his house and returned with a fifty dollar bill in his hand. When he offered it to me, I quickly refused, expressing the fact that we had plenty of wood to share and we felt we owed it to them for what they had done for us.

As I was driving back home, I struggled with second thoughts. I felt good about being able to share the extra wood with the neighbors. On the other hand, fifty dollars wasn't too much to ask for two cords of wood, and the extra money certainly was needed. I barely had enough gas in our

127

motor home to get us to our next engagement.

The first stop on our pre-Christmas tour was at Custer, South Dakota, a small town nestled in the Black Hills less than four hours from our home in Nebraska. I had received a letter from a gentleman asking us to hold a special service at the nursing home in Custer and he promised to pay us fifty dollars for conducting it. Normally, we hold services at health care facilities without charging anything; but in this case, we would be going out of our way to get to Custer and it would cost us at least fifty dollars to pay for our gas and other expenses. Because the hospital complex was situated on the edge of town, the gentleman asked us to meet him on Custer's Main Street at a prearranged time so he could then lead us there.

When we arrived, we were greeted by a small elderly man with thin, silver hair. After introducing himself, he shared with us that it was his birthday today and he had invited us to perform at the nursing home as his special gift to the staff. His wife had been ill for a long time and had just recently died. They had treated her so kindly in her last few weeks of life that he wanted to do something kind to repay them. We were, so to speak, his birthday present to them.

His old car sputtered, coughed, and smoked as we followed him to the hospital, and it left me with the impression that it probably would be a great sacrifice for the man to pay us the fifty dollars he had promised. His money might have been better spent for repairs on his car.

He had such a generous attitude and was obviously so well-liked by the staff and his friends that I found myself wishing we didn't have to take his fifty dollars. Near the end of our service, as if she had been reading my thoughts, Karen leaned over and whispered in my ear, "Tom, you know we can't take his fifty dollars."

"I know." I responded in resignation. "I feel the same way."

As we were putting away our equipment, the man stopped by with a check in his hand.

"Nice job!" he said with a smile as he handed me the check.

I took it and then quickly stuffed it back into his shirt pocket saying, "No, you don't need to pay us anything. Consider the service as our birthday present to you."

Our next meeting was at Sidney, Nebraska, about two hundred miles away. When we drove away from the hospital, we had less than a half of a tank of gasoline. Under normal conditions, our motor home would only get about six or seven miles to the gallon. Hoping to receive a miracle somewhere between Custer and Sidney, we drove on, knowing we didn't have nearly enough gas to make it that far.

When we got to Chadron, Nebraska, about a third of the way, the gas gauge showed that our tank was almost empty. I pulled into the parking lot at a truck stop and shut off the engine. This was as far as we could go unless we could get some gas.

If I had more faith, I thought to myself, *I would drive on even without any gas.* Yet the idea seemed foolish and I somehow knew if I attempted something like that, it would only result in failure and embarrassment. I sat at the driver's seat in silence wondering what to do next.

Should I give up trying to get out of debt for now and just pay for the gas by using my Visa card? I asked myself. *Perhaps when the bill arrives next month, I'll have enough money to pay it.*

Instead of wondering what we should do, or trying to think of ways to alleviate our problem, Karen sat in the

129

passenger's seat with her Bible open on her lap. She read from the fourth chapter of Mark where the account is given of Jesus presenting His Parable of the Sower. In verses eighteen and nineteen, Jesus stated: "And these are they which are sown among thorns; such as hear the word. And the cares of this world, and the deceitfulness of riches, and the lusts of other things entering in, choke the word, and it becometh unfruitful."

Considering this passage, she commented, "You know, in the past whenever I've read about the deceitfulness of riches, I always thought it was talking about people who are more interested in materialism than they are in the gospel and become distracted by it. Do you suppose it could also mean that God has already supplied everything we need, but Satan has deceived us into believing that He hasn't?

"I think you might be right!" I answered excitedly. "I may have enough money in my checking account right now to buy all the gas we need, but we don't know it. I've made mistakes with my figures before. Maybe I've made a mistake recently and have more in the account than I realize."

To make sure, I found a pay phone and called our bank. When a teller answered, I stated my name, relayed my account number, and asked her to check the balance in my account.

"I think I've made a mistake with my figures," I explained. "According to my register, I've only got two dollars and forty-seven cents left. Is that amount congruent with your figures?"

The teller was silent for a moment, and then she replied, "Sir you are right. You have made a mistake. According to our figures, you're overdrawn thirty one dollars and fifty-seven cents."

Before hanging up, I promised her I would send money to the bank as soon as possible to take care of the overdraft. Then returning to the motor home, I dejectedly reported the bad news to Karen, "Satan may have deceived us all right. But if he's hiding money from us, he's not hiding it at the bank!"

Slumping back in the driver's seat, I began pondering, once again, ways to resolve our dilemma. Kiley, who was about ten years old at that time, approached from the back of the motor home with a broad grin on her face.

"Daddy, I know what we can do!" She exclaimed. "I have some money in my piggy bank. You can use it to buy the gas you need."

Then Laura chimed in, "Me too, Daddy! You can have my money too."

Too proud to accept it, and doubting that they had enough to do much good anyway, I replied, "Thanks girls, I really appreciate your offer, but I think you need to save your money for yourselves."

But then Karen interjected her opinion: "I think you should consider their offer. You've always told the girls that they are a part of our ministry. In times of blessing, we've shared our blessings with the girls. Now we're going through a hard time, and they want to share our hard times with us too."

Still a little reluctant, I finally capitulated. "Okay, bring me your piggy banks. Let's see what you have."

To my surprise, between the two of them they had nearly twenty-two dollars. It was just enough to get us to Sidney.

The offerings received there Sidney were enough to pay my overdraft at the bank as well as some other bills. We reached our next destination — Cheyenne, Wyoming — with only about a quarter of a tank of gas.

Our service at Cheyenne was the last we had scheduled until after Christmas. We would need an unusually large offering to make it home to Nebraska, buy Christmas presents, pay bills, and survive until the beginning of our next tour — which wasn't until January. I prayed that the people would be especially generous when the offering plates were passed.

When we arrived at the church in Cheyenne, the pastor met us at our motor home door. Rather than extend his greetings, his words were: "I should have called you earlier and told you not to come. We've had a lot of trouble at this church lately and a few days ago we had a big split. Most of the people in my congregation have left and those who are still here all have the flu. I doubt if anybody will come to your service tonight! If I were you I'd just forget it."

Since we were already there and we had nowhere else to go, I talked the pastor into letting us hold the service anyway. It turned out the pastor was wrong. Seven people came to our service. Afterward, when the offering was counted, we had collected a little more than eleven dollars.

We had planned to make one last stop on our way home from Cheyenne. A half-dozen of our friends who were pastors at various churches in western Nebraska had planned to meet at a restaurant in Bridgeport, Nebraska to have dinner together and celebrate the coming of Christmas. We'd received a letter, inviting us to join them if we could. I set aside a few dollars from our offering to pay for our meal and spent the rest of it on gasoline. When we left Cheyenne, however, our gauge showed the tank was a little less than half full. It probably wouldn't be enough even to reach the Nebraska border.

Hoping there'd be a tail-wind to push us along, I carefully watched the gas gauge needle as it moved, by steady increments, toward the "empty" mark. When we reached the Nebraska border, it revealed that we had less than a quarter of a tank left. At that point, however, the needle halted its steady downward plunge. Since the needle wasn't registering movement any longer, I suspected it had gotten stuck. Without having a way to determine how much gas was left, I drove on, hoping there was enough to take us just a little further.

Finally, when it was obvious that we should have run out of gas quite awhile ago, I called Karen and the girls over to look at the gas gauge.

"Look!" I exclaimed. "The gauge says we still have almost a quarter of a tank left. We should have run out a long while ago but we're still going!"

We watched as the needle stayed where it was, still registering nearly a quarter of a tank, all the way to Bridgeport.

We had only enough money to pay for two of us at the restaurant, so Karen prepared sandwiches for the girls in the motor home. Then she and I went in to join our friends. During the meal, Rev. Ruby Long, the pastor of the Wesleyan Church in Oshkosh, Nebraska, asked us if we had plans for tomorrow's Sunday services. When we told her we didn't she invited us to follow her back to Oshkosh and attend her church.

We drove on to Oshkosh, a distance of about fifty miles, and arrived with the gas gauge still stuck at a little less than a quarter of a tank.

On Sunday morning, in the middle of the service, Mrs. Long asked us to stand and introduced us to her congregation. She talked about the work we were doing and then announced: "So now we're going to take up a special love offering for Tom and Karen." (We found out later they had been planning this offering for a number of weeks.)

The plate was passed and the treasurer brought it to me and literally dumped it into my lap. It was more than enough to fill the tank, re-supply the girls' piggy banks, buy Christmas presents, and provide us with a means to live throughout the holiday season. That offering marked the turning point in our battle to get out of debt. Several months later we achieved our goal.

Later on, I realized that I finally understood why (according to Hebrews 11:35) some people in the Bible would not accept deliverance, even though it had been provided for them. It was so "they might obtain a better resurrection".

I had, recently, had two deliverances offered to me, both in the form of fifty dollars, which I had refused. Our neighbor had offered to pay fifty dollars for the wood I delivered. I didn't accept it even though we needed it, because I wanted to be a better neighbor than that.

It had been settled and agreed upon, in our letters, that we would receive fifty dollars for the service we conducted at the hospital in Custer, South Dakota. Yet, I wouldn't accept it. Why? I wanted a better resurrection.

Finally, at Pastor Long's church in Oshkosh, Nebraska, I was offered a deliverance I did accept. I did it because so many of us could rejoice in God's goodness — those who gave and those who received.

Accepting fifty dollars for firewood or fifty dollars for a performance at a hospital might have provided just enough for us to get by. However, I chose not to accept the money and because I did, my children still remember watching as God kept our motor home running on less than a quarter tank of gas. I'm happy to have been able to share my "better resurrection" with them.

Chapter Seventeen

Family Affairs

"I wish I had someone my age to play with when we're not traveling," Laura lamented.

She had Kiley for a playmate, but Kiley was four years older and when we weren't on the road, Kiley preferred playing with her cousin, Tria. Tria was almost the same age as Kiley and lived just five miles away.

Most of the roads where we lived were merely unpaved trails across the pastures. Sometimes, when our girls were small, I would invite one of them to sit on my lap and steer the motor home. They would be delighted to sit behind the wheel while I ran the gas pedal and brake. We would drive along slowly, with me monitoring our progress, and if they happened to drive off the road and into the pasture, it didn't matter. There were no ditches, no road signs, and no trees — the only thing we could possibly hit was an occasional cow, and most of them were smart enough to get out of the way when they saw us coming.

Because of this, our girls became pretty good drivers even when they were still very young. By the time they were ten or eleven, they had the ability to drive my old International pickup truck without my assistance. Sometimes Kiley and Laura would drive to Grandma's house (just three miles away), to meet Tria (Tria also knew how to drive) and they would spend the day playing together. When they did, Laura was often the "odd man out" — not quite fitting in with the older girls and their "more grown up" ideas about how to have fun.

Laura didn't have a cousin her age like Kiley did, who

lived close by. The only people who had children she enjoyed playing with lived at least a dozen miles away.

When Laura expressed her desire to have a playmate for herself, Karen realized how unlikely that was; but instead of saying, "Forget it! That'll never happen!", she gently advised, "Laura, if you would like to have a playmate, you'll have to pray one in. That's the only way I can think of for you to have a little friend, since we live so far from anybody else."

Our girls had seen God answer our prayers on several occasions, so to Laura, asking God to send her a playmate wasn't at all outside the realm of possibility.

"I can do that!" She announced confidently, and then went up to her bedroom to get started.

That afternoon, we were surprised when we thought we heard a knock on our front door. Our house was at the end of a lane about a half mile from the road leading to the highway. When people came to visit, we usually heard them driving up — but we hadn't heard the sound of a car. Just to be sure, I looked out the kitchen window to see if there was a vehicle parked somewhere, but there wasn't.

Once again, we heard someone knocking.

When we opened the door, two little girls were standing there looking up at us.

"Can Laura come out and play? one of them asked meekly.

"Who are you? And how did you get here? Karen asked in astonishment.

"We walked over." they replied.

Then the eldest said, "My name is RaeAnne and this is my sister Becky. We've come to live with our grandparents. We heard you had a little girl named Laura and we'd like to play with her."

At that moment, Laura, overhearing the conversation, came bounding down the stairs and rushed over to greet them. In the matter of a few minutes, the three of them were chattering away as if they'd been best friends forever, and they skipped off to the back yard to play in Laura's tree house.

RaeAnne was one year older, and Becky was one year younger, that Laura. Her prayer for a friend was answered "times two".

Their father, the son of our neighbor who lived about a mile up the river, had spent most of his adult life traveling from place to place working at odd jobs. He and his wife had produced seven children over the years, and, hoping to continue their itinerate way of life, they had left their six oldest children under our neighbor's guardianship.

RaeAnne and Becky turned out to be two of the nicest, most well-behaved little girls anyone could ask for. Whenever we came home off of one of our tours, it usually wasn't long before Laura's playmates showed up, walking from their grandparent's house, to welcome her back.

*   *   *   *

It had been nearly nine years since our last baby was born when Karen and I learned we'd be having a third child. When some of our friends asked us why we had waited so long, I jokingly answered, "We just wanted to see how the first two turned out before we had another one!"

I determined to be more prepared to handle the expenses, than when Laura was born. We saved up enough money so we could afford to take the necessary time off before and after our new baby's arrival. Until that time, we stayed busy touring through Iowa, Minnesota, and the Dakotas. Because we were on tour during February and March, Karen couldn't keep regular appointments with her doctor. In early April, when the due date was still two months away, Karen came back to see him. After taking some routine tests, she noticed the doctor scowling as he surveyed the results.

"I'm afraid I have some serious concerns about your pregnancy," he informed her after a long period of study over her chart. "You have several classic symptoms of toxemia."

"What's toxemia?" Karen asked hesitantly.

"It's a condition involving the mother's blood pressure," he explained. "It seems to be more prevalent with babies that are due in the springtime or early summer, as yours is. For some reason the mother's blood pressure rises to dangerous levels. This, along with an excessively rapid gain in weight and a high level of protein found in the mother's urine, are its primary warning signs. It often leads to the loss of the baby and, in extreme cases, even to the death of the mother."

"So what's the cure?" Karen asked.

"No one has found a cure for it yet," the doctor replied somberly. "However, we will try to keep your blood pressure in check by prescribing a special diet for you to follow. Also, you must always lay and sleep on your left side from now until the baby is born."

A few days later, I was introduced to another doctor who had attended a worship service we had held at his church. Concerned about the seriousness of Karen's condition and wanting to get a second opinion, I told him about the results of her tests. He was much more straight-forward than Karen's doctor had been as he expressed his concern.

"If her blood pressure is as high as you say it is at this early stage," he warned, "you should prepare yourself for the loss of the baby and perhaps even Karen's life." Then he added, "There's a high possibility you could lose them both!"

Years earlier, when Karen was giving birth to Kiley, Psalm 121 held a special meaning for her when she read, "I will lift up mine eyes unto the hills, from whence cometh my help." Facing this new crisis, she turned again to the Scriptures for comfort and strength. For the next two months it became her primary occupation as she spent every available moment reading her Bible and meditating upon it. When she wasn't in bed lying on her side, she walked around with a Walkman cassette player hooked to her belt and headphones on her ears. She listened constantly to either the Bible on cassette or to tapes of preachers who shared positive messages of hope and faith.

Karen's doctor seemed surprised when she went back for her next checkup and her blood pressure had not increased. A couple weeks later at another checkup, the doctor acted relieved as he studied her chart.

"I don't understand how, he reported, "but your blood pressure has actually lowered significantly these last few days. Whatever it is you're doing, it seems to be working. Keep it up!"

"What I am doing," Karen replied, "is spending twenty-four hours a day in the Word."

"That's fine," he advised. "It's good if you spend a lot of time in bed reading, as long as you lay on your left side while you're doing it."

During the following weeks, as Karen continually devoted herself to the Word, her blood pressure remained low and she didn't gain any more weight. On May twenty-ninth, as Karen's pregnancy finally reached its full term, she gave birth to our third child, a beautiful and healthy baby girl we named Camilla.

Chapter Eighteen

Angels Among Us

With the addition of another member to our family, and with Kiley now a teenager, we didn't fit into our motor home as well as we had before. So we sold it and replaced it with a forty-foot, fifth-wheel trailer pulled by a customized Ford truck. During the seven years we owned the Winnebago, we drove it nearly 200,000 miles over almost every conceivable type of terrain, ranging from the broad six-lane super-highways surrounding some of America's major cities, to the narrow Sandhill cow trails found in Western Nebraska.

With our roots stemming from the Great Plains of North America and its broad expanse of level prairie, such as one finds in Kansas or in certain parts of Texas, it took some getting used to for us to adjust to mountain travel. We had a difficult time with the steep up and down terrain, and it often made us nervous when we traversed the high mountain passes.

There was one time, however, when Karen used the changes in elevation to her advantage. We were still in our motor home at the time, traveling through the mountains in Montana. She decided to bake some cream puffs and put them in the oven just as we drove across the apex of a mountain at about nine thousand feet. From there, the highway wound its way downward to six thousand feet. The change in elevation produced a corresponding change in air pressure and when Karen took her cream puffs out of the oven, they were perfect. The low air pressure at the high elevation allowed the yeast in the dough to expand excessively on the inside of the cream puffs and the higher air pressure at the lower elevation helped to create a flakey golden crust on the outside.

Shortly after we had purchased our new truck and trailer, and were traveling from Globe, Arizona to Phoenix, I decided the most direct route would be to travel through some mountains. It would take us over a winding highway, up and down some large hills, and then down a long continual grade extending several miles to the valley below. As we started down the grade, we came upon a tunnel that the highway snaked its way through. Off to our left we noticed a beautiful view of the desert valley below. Since there was a wide place between the edge of the mountain and the highway, I pulled over to get a better look.

It was time for lunch so Karen suggested, "Why don't you get your camera and take some pictures while I go back to the trailer and make sandwiches?"

It seemed like a good idea, so I took the children with me to get some shots of them with the beautiful Arizona scenery in the background while Karen prepared lunch in our fifth-wheel.

When we replaced our Winnebago with our new rig, I had some adjustments to make. The motor home, even with the equipment trailer attached, was less than forty feet long. Our new fifth-wheel trailer by itself extended to forty feet and with the truck attached we took up about the same amount of space as the semi trucks and trailers you see traveling the highways.

Our truck was a diesel powered two-and-a-half ton, customized Ford. We bought it from a horse-trailer manufacturer who refitted it specifically for the trailers he built for his customers — most of them rodeo performers or race horse owners.

Our new rig made staying on tour for months at a time

more pleasant for our growing family, but I had to learn new driving and parking techniques as we moved it from place to place. I learned to swing wide when turning corners and I became more selective about the places we parked.

Parking our motor home was simple. All I had to do was move the lever on the automatic transmission to "park" and set the brake. Parking the new truck was more complicated. I had to make sure the "two speed" was engaged, push in the clutch, and jam the gear shift lever into either a low gear or reverse — and if I didn't do it right, the truck and trailer could roll away.

Evidently I didn't get the gears to mesh quite right when we parked near the precipice overlooking the desert valley. I had parked only a short distance from a rocky cliff which was a few hundred feet to the bottom.

While preparing sandwiches, Karen noticed the trailer making some unusual creaks and groans but supposed the sounds were coming from the trailer's springs or the brakes as they cooled down. Then as she happened to look out the window, she noticed the scenery was moving. Puzzled at first, and then in a panic, as it dawned on her what was happening, she bolted out the door hoping she could out-race the truck and trailer — from the trailer's door to the truck — and stop it before it rolled over the edge of the cliff. It slowly lumbered along, driverless, picking up speed as it headed directly toward the precipice. In spite of its increasing movement, she managed to reach the truck and jump on the running board on the passenger's side. As she frantically opened the door, she discovered a stranger already seated in the driver's seat, applying the brakes and stopping the truck.

The stranger, a kindly looking gentleman who appeared to be about sixty years old, asked Karen to help him put the truck in gear and set the brake. She complied shaken yet relieved that this stranger had seemingly appeared from out of nowhere to avert this potential tragedy. The entire scene was reminiscent of something the Lone Ranger might have done in the comic books when he saved a damsel, trapped aboard a runaway train, from distress. Karen thanked him profusely for his help but still shaken, neglected to ask for his name, or why he chose to risk his life to save her from disaster.

Like the people who were rescued by the Lone Ranger but didn't think to ask "Who was that masked man, anyway?" until he was already riding off into the sunset, we've never been able to adequately recompense the stranger for his help.

He had parked his car next to our truck, shortly after we had arrived, and was exactly where he needed to be in order to climb into the driver's seat and stop it before it rolled on down the mountain. Fortunately, along with everything else I had neglected to do, I hadn't locked the doors on our truck either — so he had access to the driver's seat.

We noticed his car had a Minnesota license plate on it when he drove away. That's our only clue to his identity.

* * * *

Over the years, we've had several experiences with strangers coming to our rescue and then quietly slipping away after "saving the day" for us.

We had driven our diesel truck for a few years and began experiencing the normal mechanical wear associated with a vehicle that travels over the highways for thousands of miles. I was careful to change the oil and check the fluid levels regularly, but I didn't realize the steering mechanism needed to be greased regularly too.

One of our winter tours took us to the Northeast through some of the New England states where the highway departments use a lot of salt to keep the roads clear of ice and snow. After we had returned to Nebraska, I noticed our truck's steering didn't feel quite right. When I inspected the steering mechanism, I discovered rusty and dry joints which needed lubrication. The grease receptacles were plugged and I couldn't get my grease gun to penetrate them. Hoping a pressure-powered grease gun would take care of it, I drove to a Jiffy Lube and paid them to grease it for me. But they couldn't get it to take grease either. They advised me to take my truck to a repair shop because the steering problem was probably more serious than just a lack of lubrication.

I'd had enough experiences with mechanical repairs to know that this type of work was likely to be expensive, so when I took my truck in to be repaired, I asked for an estimate of the time and money it would take. The service manager estimated, rather flippantly, it would probably take them less than an hour to fix it and it shouldn't cost more than seventy-five dollars.

I left the truck and came back after about an hour, expecting it to be greased and ready to do. Instead, I found it with its front end jacked up and sitting on blocks. The front wheels were removed and one of the mechanics was pounding on the steering mechanism with a sledge hammer.

The service manager explained, "The steering pins are stuck worse than we first thought and we need to break them loose. Once we do that, they'll take grease and we'll get them turning again. Then he suggested, "Why don't you come back tomorrow? We should have no problem getting your truck done by then."

When I came back the next day, I found the truck still

sitting on blocks but the entire steering mechanism, along with its front axle, was missing.

"I'm afraid I have bad news for you," the service manager informed me. "Those pins were so dry and rusty we couldn't break them loose, even with a sledge hammer, so we pressed them out with a high-powered hydraulic press. They're so badly worn they'll have to be replaced — along with some other crucial parts."

It was a struggle to keep from worrying about how much all this would cost. Karen and I have a long-standing policy of not sharing our financial problems with anyone so we didn't say anything to the people at the church where we were holding meetings. I did mention to the pastor that our truck was at the repair shop being worked on, but I didn't elaborate about what was being done to it.

The only other person I talked to about it was a stranger walking down the sidewalk who stopped to visit when he saw me washing our fifth-wheel trailer.

"Do you live in this? He asked.

"Most of the time," I answered. "We have a home in Nebraska, but when we're holding special services we stay in our trailer."

"It's pretty big," he observed, "What do you use to pull it?"

I told him about our truck, mentioning that it was at the repair shop being refitted with a new steering mechanism.

After waiting another day, I went back to see how the work was progressing.

"We just finished your truck this morning," the service manager stated enthusiastically. "It's parked out back and the keys are in the ignition. It's all ready for you to just drive away."

"But what about the bill?" I asked. "Don't I need to pay

146

my bill before I can leave with my truck?"

He flipped through several sheets of paper on his clip board and then, placing one of them on top of the other, he stated, "According to my work order, the bill has already been paid. See, it says "paid in full" right across the top."

I explained to the manager that I hadn't yet paid the bill and someone must have made a mistake.

To clear up the confusion, the two of us walked back to the bookkeeping department and the service manager spoke to one of the secretaries, "Linda, what about this man's bill? According to my work order, it shows that it's already been paid."

She leafed through some of her papers, compared one of them with the work order, and said with a smile, "Yes, it's already been paid. According to our records, it's paid in full."

When I asked about how this could be so, because I hadn't paid it yet, the secretary suggested, "I think you should talk to my supervisor. He's the one who filled out the paper work on your invoice."

I immediately went to the supervisor's desk to try to clear up what I believed to be a big mistake in their accounting department.

"No," the supervisor assured me, "You don't owe us anything. Someone came by earlier this morning and paid the whole thing.

"Who was he? Why did he do it?" I asked.

"He didn't say," the supervisor replied.

I suspected that the church where we were holding meetings, or someone who attended the church, had paid my bill, so I found the pastor in his office and asked him about it.

"No," the pastor replied, "We didn't pay it. In fact, I

knew you were having some trouble with your truck, but I never bothered to find out exactly what was wrong with it."

Unsatisfied, I pressed for more answers. "What about someone from your church? Can you think of anyone who might have learned about my problem and took it upon himself to help us?"

"The pastor replied, "I suppose it's possible, but I really doubt it. Several of our people are planning a missions trip to Russia next month and we've all been stretched to the limit as far as giving is concerned. I don't know of anyone from my church who would have enough money left to pay your bill, even if they knew about it and wanted to."

So who paid the bill? Was it the stranger I'd met the day before while I was washing our trailer? Or could it have been someone who worked at the repair shop?

*　　*　　*　　*

A few years later, we had a similar incident involving mechanical problems and another stranger who came to our aid.

We stopped at an intersection waiting for the traffic light to change and suddenly our truck's engine died. I tried to restart it, but the starter wouldn't engage. Then the traffic light switched to green, so I turned on my hazard lights, but they wouldn't work either. We were suddenly "dead in the water". Every electrical component — everything depending upon electricity in our truck, had quit working. A few people in the line of cars behind us began honking their horns, signaling to us to go on through the intersection, but there was absolutely nothing I could do. With growing frustration, I frantically tried everything I'd done before, with the same lack of success. Some of the frustrated

148

motorists switched lanes and drove on around us, as the traffic light routinely turned from red to green. Before getting out of the truck to go and call a tow truck, I made one last, seemingly futile, attempt to restart our truck. Suddenly everything was back! As I turned the key, the starter engaged, my hazard lights began blinking, the engine started, and at last, we were mobile again.

As soon as I could find a safe place to pull over, I made an inspection to see what had gone wrong. I suspected that a battery cable had gotten disconnected, or shorted out, and then somehow reconnected. I didn't find anything obvious, but I went through everything anyway. I cleaned the battery terminals, tightened the connections, cleaned the starter switch, and tightened the wires on the starter.

We drove for, perhaps, a month after that without any more problems. But then one day, it did it again. This time, our truck was still in motion, so I was able to roll to a stop at a safe location. After I re-cleaned the battery terminals and rechecked the connections, everything began working again.

Just a few days later, it happened all over again. This time, it didn't seem to make any difference when I re-cleaned the terminals. Everything remained lifeless in spite of all I did. I sat back down in the driver's seat to ponder what I should try next, and suddenly everything came back on.

The system worked fine for the next two weeks. The next time it went out, however, it was at one of the worst locations possible. We were in Connecticut, bypassing New York City, traveling down a six-lane highway during the morning rush hour. Needing to refuel, I had taken an exit and stopped at a traffic light. That's when the electrical system shut down.

The people there weren't as patient as the ones had been

at the earlier traffic signal. Cars lined up behind us, the drivers honked their horns, and the line grew increasingly longer, extending back all the way onto the Interstate. We were causing a traffic jam.

I got out of the truck and wiggled the battery cables, hoping they'd somehow reengage. I was in the process of crawling under the truck to check the starter, when I heard someone nearby yell, "Get this truck out of here!"

I stood up and looked into the face of an irate policewoman. She yelled at me again, "Get this truck out of here!"

I explained, "I'm sorry, but I can't. The truck's dead in the water. There's no electricity."

As if she hadn't heard anything I'd just said, she repeated, "Get this truck out of here!"

"Ok! I'll do what I can." I promised, and started to crawl back under the truck to check the starter connection.

"Sir, get back up here!" She ordered. "It's too dangerous for you to be under there with all this traffic piled up behind you!"

Just then a tow-truck pulled up. I was still talking to the policewoman, so Karen went over to talk to the tow-truck driver.

"I can tow you out of here and take you to a real good mechanic. He's only about three miles away." he offered.

Not trusting him or his mechanic, Karen countered, "No. Just tow us over to the truck stop and leave us there."

"But lady," he pleaded, "He's a good mechanic and he can fix your truck."

"Just pull us over to the truck stop." My wife insisted. "My husband will fix our truck."

Reluctantly, he did as she asked.

Even though it was only a few hundred yards, I was

relieved that he charged us only $50 for the tow.

After re-cleaning and reconnecting the terminals, once again, the truck came back to life. We refueled and headed on down the highway making our way on through Pennsylvania and onto the Expressway traversing Ohio.

As we approached Cleveland, I felt the engine cough and lose power. I quickly realized that this time, our problem wasn't electrical. It was our fuel filters. I'd had experiences before when the filters had gotten plugged because of dirty fuel and the truck acted exactly the same.

A sign advertised a service plaza on the Expressway about ten miles ahead. We prayed that we'd make it and we did. We chugged all the way to the plaza with our engine continuously losing power.

Our truck was equipped with two fuel filters. One of them was easy to find and I could find a replacement for it at almost any auto supply store. The other was less common and I often had to put in a special order to acquire one.

I went into the station at the service plaza and asked if they had a mechanic on staff that could help me. I was told that this particular plaza didn't hire a mechanic, but the next one, fifty miles away, did. If I'd go there, I may find someone to help.

Just then, a stranger (who appeared to be a mechanic — he was wearing coveralls) walked up and announced, "I can help you. What's your problem?"

I explained that our fuel filters were plugged.

He took me inside the garage and led me to a cabinet. After he unlocked it, he asked, "Is what you need in here?"

There were only six filters on the shelf — of various shapes and sizes. To my surprise, both of the filters I needed were among them.

With his help I replaced the filters on my truck, and while

he was standing by, I went to restart the engine. I turned the key, but there was no response. The electrical system was down again.

When I explained about the recurring problem I hadn't been able to solve, he offered to see if he could come up with a solution.

He crawled underneath and after a short inspection he exclaimed, "Here's something! The grounding strap from your engine to the chasses is completely burned in two."

He went back to the garage and created a new strap out of an old battery cable that someone had discarded. After installing it, he suggested, "Now fire it up. Let's see if that worked."

It did. My electrical problems seemed to be solved.

Before closing the hood, however, the mechanic looked over my engine one more time.

"Whoa! Here's another problem!" He exclaimed. "Your alternator has a short in it."

He invited me to look, and explained, "See it making sparks once in awhile? That's probably why your grounding strap burned up. Your alternator is overloading the circuit."

He didn't have a new alternator on hand, but he promised to get me one. It was about eight o'clock on a Saturday evening and I have no idea where he found an auto supply store open at that late hour. He returned after about a half-an-hour with a new alternator.

When he had finished installing it, and I went to pay the bill, I exclaimed. "Thank you so much! How much do I owe you for all you've done for me."

"Forty-five dollars." He replied.

"What? Just forty-five dollars? The alternator, by itself, would cost more than that." I questioned.

"No. Just forty-five dollars." he repeated. "That's all I

need."

A few minutes later, as we were getting ready to pull away, he ran up to the truck with an object in his hand.

I rolled down the window to see what it was.

"You know," he said, "When you replace an alternator you're supposed to replace the voltage regulator too. The next time you stop you probably should install this." And through my open window he handed me a new voltage regulator.

Later, just out of curiosity, I went to an auto supply store and asked what the price would be on a voltage regulator like the one the stranger had given me.

They answered, "About forty-five dollars."

Who was this mysterious mechanic? Are there angels among us? I believe there are.

Chapter Nineteen

The Righteousness Suit

When we first began home-schooling Kiley in 1975, there weren't many people doing that sort of thing. The number of home-study courses available, were very limited and many of them weren't fully developed yet. Along with this, the few people before us who tried to teach their own children at home evidently hadn't been very successful. We were warned that other people more capable than we were had tried it and had failed — and held deep regrets over the consequences. Teaching our children at home, we were told, would severely limit their ability to learn, they'd become socially maladjusted, and they could never hope to be accepted by any legitimate college if, in fact, they actually completed their studies. Also Nebraska, our home state, had a reputation for persecuting parents who sent their children to Christian schools or taught them at home. Some of these people were fined and the instructors were sent to jail because their teaching methods didn't comply with the state's strict educational standards. We were very fortunate to have a County Superintendent of Schools who was a dedicated Christian. She must have overlooked some of the statutes (which were later changed through vigorous legal battles), that may have required placing our children in public schools, in order to allow us to continue traveling as a family.

Over the years we overcame the special problems that accompany teaching one's own children. As the girls grew older, they adapted to their circumstances, appearing to be at least as well-educated and as socially well-adjusted as other children who attended the public schools. However, we had no way of verifying this until after they had finished their home-study courses and left home to attend college. The lot of being our "guinea pig" fell upon Kiley, our first student. When she had finished high school but hadn't yet entered college, she struggled with mixed emotions. Part of her wanted to remain in our secure family environment while, at the same time, she had a desire to move on to the "real world" and make new friends and experience life as a "normal person". We had unwittingly placed her in a situation that put her under a lot of pressure. She knew that how she fared socially and academically during her tenure at college would be a direct reflection on us as her tutors and parents.

We also had another concern. We hadn't been able to set aside money to pay for the girls to attend college, yet we felt it was important for them to go. When our children were small, we had so many other expenditures to deal with that I had decided not to worry about college and "cross that bridge" when we came to it. When Kiley was about fifteen she began saving money on her own, putting it away in a special "college fund". By being extra frugal, she had managed to save nearly a thousand dollars by the time she finished high school.

One day, a few weeks after she had graduated, Kiley announced, "Dad, I've been praying about it and I think God wants me to buy you a new suit!"

"Whatever for?" I asked. "I have a couple of nice suits already."

"I'm not sure," she replied, "but I really do think that's what He wants me to do."

Shrugging my shoulders I responded, "Well, we'll see."

156

Although the suggestion sounded strange to me, I tried not to belittle Kiley for trying to be obedient to what she believed God wanted of her. I have observed that when someone receives a directive from the Lord such as this, usually it isn't a fleeting thing. Sometimes people — and especially teens — react on the spur of the moment to what seems to be the will of God, only to regret their actions later when the moment of inspiration has passed. However, if after a few days or weeks the impression continues to remain strong, it usually is the will of God.

Two weeks passed and throughout that time Kiley mentioned to me several times that she still believed God wanted her to buy a new suit for me. Finally I gave in, suggesting that since she had so little to spend we should try to shop at a clothing store where we could find a bargain.

There were several suits my size on the sale rack in one particular store and the prices seemed reasonable enough. It was obvious, however, that other customers had already raided the rack and the best suits were gone. I continued riffling through the leftovers, failing to notice that Kiley had left me at the sale rack. She was looking through a different rack in another part of the store. From there she called to me saying, "Dad, look here! Here's a real nice one!"

As she held it up for my inspection, I could tell that I agreed with her, even before I crossed the room. I remarked, "That is a nice suit. But I don't think it's on sale."

"It wouldn't hurt for you to try it on anyway," Kiley suggested.

While in the fitting room, I was able to locate the price tag attached to the arm of the coat. The price was way too high. *Well, that settles that!* I thought to myself. *There's no way I'm going to let Kiley spend that kind of money for a new suit.* Even so, I stepped out of the fitting room wearing

157

the suit, intending to suggest to Kiley that we go look somewhere else.

As soon as she saw me, Kiley stated enthusiastically, "Wow, it looks great on you! I have to buy you that suit!"

"But wait a minute, honey!" I protested. "I don't think you should! First of all, the pants don't fit me quite right."

Right then a store clerk interrupted me (just as I was about to make my second point). She said, "Oh, that's all right sir. We have a tailor in the store and she can make them fit."

"Do it then!" Kiley ordered, and I was escorted off to the tailor who began measuring the pants and then marking them with straight-pins, customizing a perfect fit. At the same time, Kiley wrote out a check, paying for the suit out of her college fund. When we left the store, I carried a fancy box under my arm, containing an almost tailor-made suit. I was extremely chagrined because I had allowed my daughter to pay for it when she really couldn't afford to.

In the years following, that suit came to represent more to me than just something nice to wear when I dressed up. It also depicted my daughter's sacrifice, obedience, and love. I first became aware of this after Kiley had been in college for about two years.

Like most men when they reach middle age — especially in their early forties — I gradually began gaining more and more weight. One day I put on my suit and discovered the tailor-made pants didn't fit anymore. For months, my wife had been warning me that my "spare tire" seemed to be inflating, but for the most part I simply ignored her. *What's the difference!* I rationalized. *Most men don't look good anymore after they turn forty anyhow — whether they're fat or not!* Now, however, it seemed that my self-indulgence at the dinner table had finally caught up to me and I was forced to make a decision. Either I would have to go on a diet, change my eating habits and lose some weight, or I would never be able to wear my special suit again.

For me, dieting takes discipline and I need an extra incentive to stay with it. Once my hunger reaches the point that it seems almost overwhelming, it's easy to rationalize, *after all, I'm not as fat as most men my age. So what if I weigh twenty pounds more than I did ten years ago. I still don't look too bad.* But that day I was forced to conclude, even if that was true, I would still have to forget about wearing Kiley's suit.

Not once over the years has Kiley ever asked, "Are you still wearing my suit?" She doesn't demand that I wear it and hasn't even asked me to treat it with respect. However, it doesn't seem right to me if I don't   When I consider what she sacrificed to buy it, it isn't too much to ask to just stay on my diet until I finally fit into the suit again. In other words, Kiley's gift not only makes me look good when I wear it, it's the incentive I need to keep myself in the kind of shape that makes the suit look good as well.

I've used my suit as an illustration of the righteousness of Christ in some of my sermons. Romans 5:17 states; "For if by one man's offense death reigned by one; much more they which receive abundance of grace and of the gift of righteousness shall reign in life by one, Jesus Christ." This verse reveals that God offers righteousness to us as a gift.

I Corinthians 5:21 also reveals: "For he hath made him to be sin for us, who knew no sin; that we might be made the righteousness of God in him."

Sometimes I explain this verse by referring to my suit: Suppose that someone were to give you a brand new suit. It was clean and spotless to begin with, but one day, through your own carelessness, you put a stain on it. Later on, you

159

ripped the trousers. At another time you burned a hole in the coat. Eventually, through all your carelessness, your new suit became torn, tattered, and filthy. It's now an embarrassment to you because it reveals your lack of self-control and thoughtlessness. You must keep wearing it, however, because it's all you have.

Then one day, through some miracle, you are invited to meet the king, the ruler of your country. You are thrilled to be so honored, but are also embarrassed because your clothing reveals your low estate, your mistakes, and your lack of discipline. You realize you aren't worthy to meet the king in such a filthy condition. But then you meet a stranger who learns of your predicament and offers to swap clothing with you. The suit he is wearing is resplendently white and bears no stain, tear, or wrinkle whatsoever. It's hard to imagine, but somehow, even though the stranger lives in the same filthy world under the same lowly conditions that you're living in, his suit doesn't reveal it at all. He has successfully avoided all the things that have stained and torn your suit.

When you stand before the king wearing the stranger's suit, he and his servants treat you with the utmost honor and regard. They respect you greatly because your suit reveals that you are a person of discipline and wisdom. The stranger, on the other hand, cannot stand before the king as you do at all. He isn't allowed to associate with people of your status because he's wearing your filthy rags. People accuse him of being lazy, careless, and undisciplined.

How would you treat a suit that was given to you under those conditions? Even though Jesus doesn't demand it, I am compelled to treat his gift of righteousness with the same kind of respect I might give to the stranger's suit — doing everything I can to measure up to the stature of the man who gave it to me. Whenever His suit doesn't fit me anymore, I don't try to change the suit — I change myself, the man wearing the suit.

Incidentally, I kept on wearing Kiley's suit, especially on special occasions, for many years afterward. Because it looked good on me, I made sure that I looked good in it.

As far as Kiley's plans to attend college were concerned, Karen and I encouraged her to go in spite of the fact that the money she had saved wasn't even enough to pay for her books, let alone the college tuition.

As it turned out, however, Kiley was a very good student, maintaining a 4.0 average throughout the time she spent in college. As a result, she received scholarships and grants, virtually eliminating her need to pay tuition.

One day, just out of curiosity, I gathered my canceled checks and receipts and calculated the exact amount it had cost me, personally, to send Kiley to college. At that time, she was in her third year. The total amounted to less than twenty-seven hundred dollars. That averages out to be just nine hundred dollars per year. As I considered how little it had cost, I exclaimed to Karen, "I think it would be wise for us to try to keep Kiley in school for as long as we can. We can't keep her at home for what it costs us to send her to college!"

Chapter Twenty

The Word and the Witness

About five years after Camilla was born, I woke up one morning with a vivid memory of a strange dream I'd had during the night. It was about a rat that had somehow gotten into our house, but it didn't have the appearance of a rat. Instead, it was white and fluffy and had eyes like a little kitten. In spite of its benevolent appearance, Karen was terrified of it and wanted me to kill it — which I reluctantly attempted. I had a lot of difficulty doing so, however.

The dream had such an impact on me that, as I was getting dressed, I commented to Karen, "Boy, I had the oddest dream last night!"

She chuckled at my comment and replied, "It must have been something we both ate for supper last night because I had a really strange dream too."

Curious, because Karen doesn't usually remember having dreams, I asked, "Really, what was it about?"

"It was about a strange white rat," she replied. "Even though it was cute and fluffy, for some reason I was scared of it and wanted someone to kill it for me."

I couldn't believe what I had just heard. Both of us woke up that morning with memories of the same dream. Karen was equally amazed as I filled in the details of her dream for her, describing each aspect of the rat she had seen and how kitten-like it had appeared. As we compared our dreams, however, we found that though most of the details paralleled each other, the outcomes were different. In her dream, Karen asked her father to kill the rat, but even though he tried, he couldn't find anything to kill it with. In my dream, it was me that Karen had asked to kill it, but the only thing I could find for a weapon was a leather strap. I felt terrible killing the cute little creature in such a horrible manner. Yet I felt compelled to do so because I knew that, even though the creature had the appearance of a kitten, it actually wasn't. In reality, on the inside, it was still a big, ugly rat.

Having so many parallel details in both of our dreams made us suspect that God had a message for us. But what was it? What was the symbolism hidden within these dreams?"

After careful consideration we concluded that the white, kitten-like rat represented the devil. He has the ability to appear as an angel of light but in reality is our enemy. In spite of its outward façade, our kitten-like creature was still a rat on the inside. In her dream, Karen wasn't fooled by its benign appearance — she wanted someone to kill it, yet seemed unable to do so herself.

Her father's willingness to help her, yet inability to do so, expressed a warning from God that Karen would be facing a satanic attack which would require help from others to overcome. The fact that her father couldn't do it indicated that she wouldn't find her answers from traditional sources. As a child, her father had lovingly nurtured and protected her and Karen instinctively ran to him whenever she was in trouble. However, repelling this kind of attack would require more than just a father's natural inclination to protect his children when they are in danger.

The elements of my dream suggested that I would find a way to defeat Karen's adversary, but it wouldn't be easy. I remember being frustrated because I couldn't find something to use that was more lethal. I felt terrible having to whip the creature to death with only a leather strap, but it was the only weapon available. To me, the leather strap has a special meaning because it was the instrument used to flog Jesus before He was nailed to the cross. Isaiah 53:5 alludes to its significance by stating: "— by His stripes we are healed."

A few months later when Karen went to the doctor for a routine check-up, her tests revealed an ominous threat. In retrospect I'm convinced it related directly to the warning we'd received through our parallel dreams. Before revealing the results of the tests, the doctor called us both into her office and then spoke to Karen in a very solemn and serious manner.

"I would like to schedule you for a hysterectomy right away. Our tests reveal that you have something growing inside you where it shouldn't be. It might be either a fibroid tumor or it could be a cancer — and personally, I don't think it's a fibroid tumor."

She went on to explain that the reason she suspected the tumor was cancerous was because of its rapid growth and its irregular shape.

Although the doctor pressed us to set up an appointment with the hospital and surgeon immediately, we decided to wait — choosing instead to take some time to pray about the situation before we did anything at all. We had learned, years before, that God always seems to have plenty of time to do whatever He chooses to do. As His children, we should also have time to spare. In fact, of all of God's creation, the devil seems to be the only one short on time. The rest of us have an eternity awaiting us. Because of this, it isn't our policy to make important decisions on the spur of the moment.

On the way home from the clinic, Karen confided, "If I must submit to a hysterectomy, I'd just as soon have it done by a specialist. I'm going to make an appointment with a gynecologist and get a second opinion."

There aren't many doctors in our remote corner of Nebraska and the closest gynecologist was at North Platte, about one hundred and seventy-five miles from our home. Before making the call, Karen fervently prayed that God would guide her to make contact with exactly the right doctor, someone she could place confidence in.

She dialed the office of Dr. Dellinger one of the gynecologists listed in the telephone book and asked his receptionist if she could set up an appointment with him.

"Yes, I believe we have an opening for you," the receptionist replied. And then she suggested a date and time, only a couple of days away.

It wasn't until a week or two later that we became aware of how unusual it was to have scheduled this appointment with Dr. Dellinger. One of his nurses, curious because she knew Karen wasn't one of his regular patients, asked her how she happened to be accepted by him.

"I just called his receptionist and asked for an appointment," Karen replied. "Why?"

"I can't believe that!" the nurse replied. "There's a waiting list of people as long as your arm trying to get in to see Dr. Dellinger. Yet you tell me you made an appointment with him just by making a random phone call. That is very unusual."

Dr. Dellinger was a soft-spoken man in his sixties, and his confident manner put Karen's mind at ease almost immediately. After his examination, he assured her that he was almost certain her problem wasn't cancer, but only a benign fibroid tumor. He strongly recommended that she have a hysterectomy, but told her as healthy as she seemed and as young as she looked, surviving the surgery should be a "piece of cake" for her. Therefore, we scheduled an appointment for her to have surgery in a couple of weeks.

In spite of Dr. Dellinger's reassurances, Karen wasn't anxious to submit to this operation. First of all, she was scheduled to speak at a women's conference in about a month but she decided not to cancel it because of her physical problems. Secondly, she remembered visiting with several women we'd met on our tours who described the trauma of this type of surgery and how it had taken them, literally, months to recover. Thirdly, we didn't have health insurance and we hadn't set any money aside for an expense such as this. We weren't sure what a hysterectomy would cost, but realized it would be several thousand dollars. Finally, Karen had never been in a situation before where she would be placing her life in someone else's hands, and yet wouldn't be able to pray for herself because she would be asleep during the operation. She was haunted by the thought of the doctor or anesthetist making a deadly mistake during surgery. I tried to console her with the fact that, while she was anesthetized, our girls and I would be praying.

For the next several days, Karen struggled in a mental battle, imagining an unforeseen tragedy taking place during the operation, countered by God's promises of protection over her found in the Bible. Sometimes, even while preoccupied with a household chore, a horrible mental image of a bizarre surgical disaster would suddenly spring to her mind, leaving her shaken and weak. It was clearly an encounter of the warfare described in II Corinthians 10:3—5: "For though we walk in the flesh, we do not war after the flesh: (For the weapons of our warfare are not carnal, but mighty through God to the pulling down of strong holds.) Casting down imaginations, and every high thing that exalteth itself against the knowledge of God, and bringing into captivity every thought to the obedience of Christ."

Karen voiced her frustrations to me one day saying, "I

know what the Word says about healing. I know Jesus was manifested to bring deliverance and healing to all of mankind. I have many verses relating to these things memorized. My problem is getting my spirit to agree with the promises that I know are in the Word. Because of my fears, I haven't been able to get a witness from God telling me that this surgery isn't even necessary."

In response, I suggested, "What can you get a witness about? Are you comfortable believing God will protect you so that there won't be any surgical complications?"

She replied, "Yes."

"How about this too:" I continued, "Can you believe God for a rapid recovery so that by the time you're supposed to speak at the women's conference you'll be feeling fine?"

"Yes, I wouldn't have any trouble agreeing with you about that either," she answered.

"Okay," I pressed further. "Do you think you can see yourself in the aftermath of the operation, recovering without any pain?"

"Yes," she replied, "I can picture God doing that for me too."

"All right then." I proposed, "Until you get something more definite from the Lord, let's believe Him for that much at least."

I set aside the ten days prior to when she was scheduled for surgery to fast and pray. Although I didn't ask it of them, our three girls chose to fast and pray during this time as well. The day before Karen's surgery, as I was discussing with the girls what I was most impressed to pray about, I mentioned that I was asking God for a successful operation and a quick, painless recovery.

Kiley replied, "That's great Dad, because I've been most impressed to pray that God will supply all the money you need to pay for the operation. I'm praying that every bill will be paid without borrowing the money."

Then Laura shared the crux of her most specific petition. "I've been praying that Mom will finally win this spiritual battle that Satan has been waging with her."

"It sounds like we have just about every aspect of this problem covered!" I suggested.

Karen's mental battles intensified as the date of the surgery grew nearer. On the morning the operation was scheduled, she was silent most of the way as we drove to North Platte. This concerned me because Karen usually does a lot of talking when she is nervous or excited. As she was sitting on the hospital bed, being prepared for surgery, I noticed she was trembling uncontrollably.

As terrified as she is now, what will she be like once she gets to the operating room? I wondered to myself.

Soon a nurse appeared with a wheel chair. We prayed a short prayer together, I kissed her goodbye, and she was whisked away.

Evidently, time slows down in hospital waiting rooms. It seems to happen every time I enter one. Eventually I received word that Karen's surgery was over. Dr. Dellinger greeted me with his usual confidence, telling me that everything had gone well. He had found and removed a lump about the size of a grapefruit near her ovaries — which he had sent to the lab to be tested — but it appeared that it wasn't cancerous and he didn't think we had anything to be concerned about.

When I was given the "go ahead" to see Karen in the recovery room, I entered expecting her to be groggy from the after-effects of the anesthesia. Instead, she was sitting in bed laughing and smiling, swapping jokes with her anesthetist. A short while later, the telephone next to her bed rang and

Karen answered it. It was a friend who had heard Karen was having surgery and called to see how things had gone. The friend was surprised when it was Karen who answered the phone. As they chatted, the focus of the conversation changed from how things were going with Karen to her friend's personal problems. I listened as Karen shared encouraging Scriptures and counsel about what her friend could do to help her wayward son.

Finally, after the anesthetist had left and the phone conversation was over, I commented, "Well, you seem to be feeling pretty good! I expected you to still be groggy from the anesthesia."

"No," Karen replied. "I feel fine!"

"What happened?" I asked. "When I left you, you were shaking like a leaf."

Karen explained, "Well, once I reached the operating room, I decided that since I was placing my life in the doctor's and the anesthetist's hands, they would probably do a lot better job on me if they liked me. So I started making jokes and being friendly to win them over. I guess it worked!"

"I guess it did!" I observed. "The anesthetist couldn't wait for you to wake up so he could continue your banter back and forth."

We visited for awhile and then a nurse entered the room stating, "I have a hypo to give you for your pain."

Karen responded, "Thank you, but I'm not feeling any pain. I feel a little downward pressure on my abdomen, but that's all. No pain."

The nurse looked at her askance and then asked, "Are you sure? I would think you would be in quite a lot of pain by this time."

Still doubtful, the nurse left the room. Before she did, she showed Karen where the button was to alert the nurse's station and told her to call whenever the pain finally hit and she needed the hypo.

An hour or so later, the nurse reentered the room with a look of determination on her face. "I don't care whether you're asking for it or not," she stated flatly, "you're getting a hypo! The doctor ordered me to give one to you."

Other than a sense of downward pressure on her abdomen that eventually abated, and the stab of the stiff surgical thread around the incision that poked and pulled once in awhile, Karen felt no discomfort in the aftermath of the surgery. She was released from the hospital on the following afternoon and had recovered completely by the time of the woman's conference a few weeks later.

The day before we left to travel to North Platte for Karen's surgery, my mother (who wanted to help) gave me a check for one thousand dollars and told me to apply it toward the hospital bill. Soon after I checked Karen in, I met with the hospital's financial administrator and gave her the check. Although I wasn't sure where the money would come from, I promised to send another check for three thousand dollars within three months, and then pay three thousand dollars every six months until the bill was paid.

At this time, our ministry's finances paid for itself, but it was rare for us to have anything extra. Paying for Karen's surgery within two-and-a-half months would have seemed like an impossibility if someone would have told me that that's what would happen. We didn't mention to people how much the surgery cost or that we weren't covered by insurance. Yet, somehow, the money came in and every bill was paid. Every time I received a statement relating to her operation, I had the means to pay that particular one. I received the first bill, one from her anesthetist, about two weeks after the surgery. Although it was nearly all we had, I had enough money in our account to pay it, so I did. A few days later, I received the statement for the cost of the operation room. In the meantime, we had received a generous offering from one of the churches where we were holding meetings. Since I, once again, had enough money, I paid it too. The statements arrived at staggered intervals. Whenever they came, I always had just enough to pay them.

I had made an agreement with the hospital's financial administrator that I would make our first three thousand dollar payment on January fifteenth. But because I'd already paid the bills whenever I was first notified of them, I didn't have to make any three thousand dollar payments. When January fifteenth came, the entire bill had already been paid in full.

Chapter Twenty One

Love and Marriage

When Kiley went off to college, she chose a small school in a rural community — Friends Bible College at Haviland, Kansas.

Four years later, shortly before Laura left home, she announced, "I've been all over America and I've traveled to almost every state in the Union. When I go to college, I'd like to go somewhere I've never been before. I want to go to school in Canada."

She had watched a mini-series on television entitled *Ann of Green Gables* and was impressed with the beautiful scenery portrayed in the film. Much of it was filmed on Prince Edward Island located in the Atlantic Maritimes. When she learned about a Bible college in nearby Sussex, New Brunswick, she decided that she wanted to go there.

As it had been before with Kiley, we weren't able to save up enough money to send Laura to college. Along with that, attending college in a different country would disqualify her from receiving government grants and loans. After contacting the college, we learned that the school only gave its limited number of scholarships to Canadian citizens. Also, the distance from our home in Nebraska to the college in New Brunswick is over twenty-five hundred miles. Buying airline tickets to get Laura there and back home again, in itself, was likely to be quite expensive.

Considering the reality of our condition, yet trying not to discourage her, I outlined the situation to her. "This is likely to cost a lot of money we don't have at the moment. If you really want to go to school in Canada, I'll need your help in praying in the funds so we can do it."

Our shortage of money didn't seem to deter Laura's enthusiasm and during the following weeks, she excitedly shared her plans to attend college in Canada with her family and friends. Apparently, she never questioned that God would provide the money somehow.

One afternoon, my father called and asked if it was really true that I was going to send my daughter all the way to New Brunswick, in Canada, to attend a Bible college. Before I answered, I braced myself to hear him express his disapproval because, even after all these years, he still indicated his disappointment, from time to time, about my choice of occupation. I had left the ranch to travel in full time ministry and now my daughters seemed to be following in my footsteps.

When I had told him that it was true, to my complete surprise, he announced, "Well then, I've decided to pay for it."

Not sure I had heard him right, I asked him to repeat what he had just said.

True to his promise, my father paid for her college — her tuition, her airline tickets, and even some of her personal expenses.

Wearing a cowboy hat while holding her favorite teddy bear under her arm, Laura boarded the plane at the airport in Omaha, heading for her destination in New Brunswick. After the plane had taken off, Karen, Cami, and I watched from the terminal, tracking the vapor trail as the airliner gained altitude and finally faded out of sight.

A wealthy businessman, who was also seeing a daughter off to college (his was returning to an ivy-league school in new-England), noticed us still gazing into the sky and asked, "So, is this your daughter's first year away from home?"

"Yes," we replied sullenly.

"Where's she going?" he inquired further.

"Sussex, New Brunswick, Canada," I answered.

He shook his head and commented quietly, "I'm glad I'm not the one who'll be paying your phone bills."

* * * *

Unlike most teenage girls, Laura wasn't particularly interested in dating or having boyfriends, especially during her early teenage years. This was probably due to the fact that we hardly ever stayed in one place long enough for her to develop any deep friendships. Laura seemed to enjoy her independence and often expressed her intention to remain single, at least throughout her twenties, so she would be free to pursue her private plans and ambitions without anyone's interference. Because of this, Karen and I were a little surprised when she began talking more and more, in her letters to us, about a particular friend of hers at college named Jason.

Jason was a senior, majoring in both music and pastoral ministry. He was talented and intelligent, with a particular gift for playing the piano. His home was Moncton, New Brunswick, a small city on the Atlantic coast where approximately a third of the population who live there are of French descent. Therefore, Jason was bilingual, able to speak both English and French.

At first, Laura insisted that she and Jason were nothing more than just good friends. However, after a few months, she finally admitted that they were dating and her feelings toward him had grown beyond those of mere friendship.

One day, in the spring, about two weeks before Jason's graduation, I received a phone call from him asking for my blessing upon his proposal of marriage to Laura.

I jokingly replied, "I might consider it, if you'll give me fifteen cows for her."

Jason ignored my quip and repeated his request without commenting about the fifteen cows at all. Evidently he considered the whole matter too serious to joke about.

They were married the following January on a cold winter day. The temperatures by mid-afternoon that day climbed to almost zero Fahrenheit. At that time, Jason was employed as a youth pastor and music leader at a church in Winchester, Ontario. After a short honeymoon in sunny Florida, they flew to frigid Ontario to begin spending the rest of their lives together.

Meanwhile, Kiley (four years older than Laura) was still single. Years before, when Kiley was eighteen and traveling with us, one of our meetings was at a small church in Hamilton, Montana. One of the people in the audience was particularly impressed by Kiley's mannerisms and personality. Later that evening, he called his son in Oklahoma (who was attending Bible College at Bartlesville, preparing for the ministry). "Son," he suggested, "I think I've just met the girl that will be my daughter-in-law someday. Her name is Kiley Cobb and I think she'll make a perfect wife for you."

"Yeah, right!" Michael (his son) answered derogatorily, "Do you think any person alive would actually be interested in a girl that his father picked out for him?"

At the close of Kiley's third year of school in Kansas, she was informed that the college had decided to drop music as one of its majors. Therefore, if Kiley wanted to graduate with a degree in music, she would have to transfer to a different school. Because of this, she decided to take a year's sabbatical and not enroll at another college until later.

She used that time to pursue her ambition of becoming a professional gospel singer. For ten months, working as her own agent, Kiley lined up an itinerary of concerts and special performances throughout the Midwest.

One of her performances was at a church in Syracuse, Kansas where she was the featured performer at a Christian youth rally. The young pastor who organized the event and arranged to have Kiley perform was Michael, the son of the gentleman from Montana. By this time he had graduated from college and was now living in Syracuse, working as an associate pastor. After he had finally met her, Michael began considering more seriously what his father had told him a few years earlier.

The next fall, Kiley went back to school, enrolling at Bethany Bible College in Sussex, New Brunswick — the same college Laura had attended. In the spring, Kiley sent her resume to several organizations hoping first of all, to find a position as a vocalist with a professional musical group or, if that didn't work out, as a music director or song leader at a church. One of the churches that received her resume was the Wesleyan Church in Syracuse, Kansas. After reading it, Pastor Rodney Collins (the senior pastor) promptly called a meeting of his administrative board and acquired their approval to offer Kiley a job for the summer.

Pastor Collins had known Kiley since she was a little girl. Over the years, our family had held meetings for him at the churches he served.

One evening, shortly after he had offered Kiley a position at his church, he and his wife were lying in bed getting ready to go to sleep. He sat up on an elbow and said, "Julie, something's bothering me and I need to clear it up before I can get to sleep. Do you think I would have offered Kiley that job at the church if she wasn't single and I didn't think she would make a good wife for Michael, our youth pastor?"

Julie responded, "Well, to be perfectly honest with you, I doubt if you would have."

Turning over and yawning, he replied, "Thank you, Julie. I just needed to make sure."

Kiley's office at the church was right next to Michael's. Therefore, courtesy required that they acknowledge each other at least a half dozen times a day. Before long, they fell in love and by August, Michael had asked Kiley to marry him.

As I performed their wedding ceremony in November, I assured the congregation that Michael and Kiley's union wasn't actually an "arranged marriage"; but because of the involvement of Pastor Collins and Michael's father, it came awfully close.

Chapter Twenty Two

Joining Forces

From the onset of our traveling ministry, it was never very difficult for us to find enough to do. When Kiley and Laura were still in their teens and Cami was a toddler, our ministry seemed to generate the most response. This was probably due to our close family relationship which lent credibility to our message.

When Kiley and Laura left home to pursue their own specific callings from God, we noticed it becoming more and more difficult to schedule future meetings and large gaps of open time appeared in our schedule.

During our ministry's heyday, Karen and I had entertained hopes that it would continue to expand as our children grew older and by the time they were adults, there would be enough income and work for all of us. After Kiley and Laura went away, it seemed we would have to abandon those dreams. Jason and Laura had moved from Ontario to Williston, North Dakota, and were comfortably settled there working as music leaders and youth pastors at a dynamic and growing church. Michael and Kiley planned to stay at Syracuse, Kansas, to continue the work that Michael had started there.

A few days before Michael and Kiley's wedding, I parked our RV at their church so we would be close and could help Kiley make the final preparations for the wedding ceremony. When Jason and Laura arrived from North Dakota to share this happy time with us, they opted to stay with us in our fifth-wheel trailer, rather than rent a room at a motel. A typical recreational vehicle, our trailer's limited space was designed to transform to accommodate multiple functions. There was only one small bedroom which temporarily became Jason and Laura's private space. Cami slept at the trailer's dinette which we converted into a single bed at night. Karen and I slept on the living room couch which we transformed into a double bed.

In the morning, as Jason and I were sharing a pot of coffee before breakfast, I commented, "Wouldn't it be fun if we could just keep right on living this way?"

I was speaking "tongue in cheek", expecting Jason to groan at the suggestion. Jason (who is six feet three inches tall) had just struck his head on the air conditioner shroud as he was pouring himself a cup of coffee. It was evident he hadn't spent much time in a camper, nor had he ever tried to live in such cramped quarters with so many other people. Obviously, he was having some trouble adjusting to our special style of living.

To my surprise he responded, "I'd love it! I can't think of anything else I'd rather do."

"Are you serious?" I asked. "I thought you probably hated living like this."

Laura had been eavesdropping from the bedroom and suddenly appeared, dressed in her bathrobe — yawning, yet looking bright-eyed and excited.

"Do you mean it Dad?" she asked. "You really wouldn't mind if Jason and I joined up with you to travel full time?"

"Of course I wouldn't mind," I replied. "But it would take a lot of faith on everyone's part to pull it off."

For the next hour, as I turned Cami's bed back into a dinette and Karen prepared breakfast, we talked about what each of us might have to offer in such a corporate undertaking and what adjustments would have to be made. Although I didn't mention it, I struggled in my mind over the financial difficulties that inevitably would follow such an arrangement. If Karen and I were barely making ends meet as things were, how could our ministry possibly support the addition of another two members? However, since Jason and Laura had just recently moved to North Dakota and were content there, I set my concerns aside figuring it would be at least ten years before they were actually ready to join forces with us as a ministry team.

Immediately after they returned to North Dakota, however, Jason and Laura became more and more discontent with their situation there. As the weeks went by, issues of contention arose between them and their pastor, and finally, in early January, Jason submitted his resignation.

Late one evening, I received a phone call from Laura. She asked hesitatingly, "Do you remember our conversation in November when we discussed the possibility of joining up with you in the ministry? Well, Jason and I have been talking it over and if you and Mom are willing, we'd like to do it now."

Trying not to betray my concerns about the financial pressures that this would entail, I replied, "Great! Karen and I have been talking it over too, and we'd be happy to have you."

Our ministry was in the worst slump of its entire twenty-two year history. It seemed to be the worst possible time for us to take on this new responsibility. On the other hand, I realized it might be just what we needed to bring us out of it.

I had nothing scheduled until March and the money we had set aside to get by on until we were back on tour was dwindling rapidly. Also when we were finally able to get back on the road, most of the churches that had scheduled us were small and probably wouldn't pay us much. On the positive side, however, these two open months would give us the time we needed to move Jason and Laura from North Dakota to Nebraska and get them settled in the upstairs of our house. (They would live there until they could afford to buy or rent their own home.) We could spend the rest of this time forming our ministry team.

Another concern was the strength of our family unit. Looking back to the time when we were first married, neither Karen nor I could imagine living and working with our own in-laws on a twenty-four hour-a day basis. Even though we loved our parents, we probably couldn't have lived with them without becoming annoyed by their individual idiosyncrasies. I knew of several instances where happy families seemed to get along just fine until they tried working together in partnership. Once a rift had developed and they had broken apart, they were never able to reconcile their differences again.

On the other hand, Karen and I believed that having Jesus at the center of the home is the key to having successful family relationships.

An outstanding example of the impact that Jesus can make upon people is illustrated by the types of individuals He chose for his twelve disciples. They were an eclectic group made up of fishermen, businessmen, a tax collector, and a Zealot.

Matthew, the tax collector, would have been labeled a traitor to his nation, at that time. The Romans (who were considered heathens by the Jews) had, years before, defeated the Jewish army and placed its citizens in subservience, occupying the nation and demanding tribute. Rather than take on the disdainful task of collecting taxes from the resentful citizens themselves, they offered attractive financial rewards to anyone who was willing to do it for them. Since Matthew had been willing to collect taxes for the Romans, he probably was the type of person who would sell his grandmother into slavery if he could make a profit on the deal. Politically, the Publicans (tax collectors) were in league with their national enemies.

The antithesis of the Publicans, were the Zealots. A Zealot was someone who had become so disenchanted with the Roman system that he was willing to do almost anything to subvert it. Since they couldn't defeat the Romans openly, they worked underground, inflicting damage whenever they could by committing sabotage and assassinations. One of Jesus' disciples was a Zealot (Luke 5:15 and Acts 1:13). His name was Simon (he was a different Simon than the one referred to as Simon Peter).

When you consider the affiliation of these two people and what each of them stood for, it's amazing to find references in the Bible to them even being in the same room — let alone living and working together on a continual basis. Yet Matthew and Simon both followed Jesus for three-and-a-half years. Apparently, Jesus created harmony between these two political opposites. In today's world, it would be like appointing the most conservative Republican and the most liberal Democrat to work on the same committee and then ask the two of them to balance the federal budget.

If Jesus can bring unity between a Publican and a Zealot, it shouldn't be a problem for Him to create harmony among family members — even between parents, daughters, husbands, wives, and in-laws.

When March came, all of us packed our belongings into the trailer and began our first tour, traveling to Kansas, Arkansas, Indiana, Ohio, Pennsylvania, New York, and into Canada — first to Ontario, and then to New Brunswick.

Our tour wasn't over until the middle of June, and during that time we endured blizzards, flat tires, a stalled truck on the outskirts of New York City, steep narrow mountain trails, and a myriad of other things that might have set us at odds with each other. Yet we survived as a family unit and the foundation of our ministry as a team had been set. We enjoyed ourselves so much that we all hated to see the tour come to an end.

After Jason and Laura joined up with us, I had hoped people would recognize that there were added expenses involved in maintaining a ministry which included two families and would respond accordingly. I was quite surprised when they didn't — at least not during our first year together. Yet somehow, we were able to pay our bills and meet our expenses anyway.

At the close of our first year as a team, I calculated our income for that year and compared it to our previous year's income. The separate totals were almost exactly the same. Yet during that year none of us realized that our income was so deficient. When bills were due, we were able to pay them. When we needed money for extra expenses it was always available.

Chapter Twenty Three

"Ka-chunk, Ka-chunk"

Jason and Laura traveled in our truck and lived with us in our trailer for nearly a year. Then they purchased a small used mini-home of their own for only thirty-three hundred dollars. Considering that new mini-homes may sell for more than twenty times that much, we considered that finding one for that price was another miracle.

We began our Winter/Spring tour with high hopes and the anticipation of new doors and unexplored avenues of ministry opening before us. We had a lot of quick stops planned throughout Kansas, Colorado, Oklahoma, and Texas, before we traveled east to Georgia, north to Indiana, and then west again. There were a few gaps in our schedule, but we hoped to fill them while we were on the road.

We soon discovered the advantage of having two traveling rigs. Early into our tour, Karen and I had a breakdown with our trailer. We were in Kansas and had a service scheduled in Colorado, about a hundred miles away, so we loaded our equipment in Jason and Laura's mini-home and sent them (with Cami) on ahead.

I found a welding shop to make the repairs, and because the welders were so efficient, we had our trailer securely reattached and ready to go in just a few hours. Karen and I made it to our destination with only about ten minutes to spare. However, Jason, Laura, and Cami had arrived hours earlier, getting everything set up, and we started the service right on time.

A few weeks later, we were traveling from a meeting in northeastern Oklahoma to our next engagement which was near Waco, Texas. However, about fifteen miles north of McAllister, Oklahoma, the engine in our diesel truck suddenly began vibrating violently, making a "ka-chunk, ka-chunk" sound. The grinding noise of metal hitting against metal made me realize that something inside had broken loose. I immediately shut it off and let the truck and trailer coast to a stop. Aware that something was seriously wrong, I didn't try to restart it. Instead I had Jason and Laura take me on to McAllister where I could find a tow truck and a diesel mechanic.

During the trip to town, I recalled a promise found in Psalm 37: "The steps of a good man are ordered by the Lord; and he delighteth in his way. Though he fall, he shall not be utterly cast down; for the Lord upholdeth him with his hand." (Psalm 37:23, 24) I soon found myself praying, *Lord direct my steps as I look for someone to help me during this situation.*

We found a wrecker service near the edge of McAllister and I made arrangements with them to retrieve our truck and trailer from the side of the roadway. While at their office, I leafed through the yellow pages in a phone book looking for a diesel mechanic; but none that I called had any open time and wouldn't be able to look at our truck and diagnose its problem for at least two or three days.

Not sure where to have our rig towed, I asked the driver if he had any suggestions about where I could find an available diesel mechanic.

"There's a big diesel garage here in McAllister that does a lot of business with the truckers that come through. You might try them." he suggested.

Feeling an unexplained uneasiness about following this advice, I asked, "Suppose it was your truck that was making "ka-chunk, ka-chunk" noises and you weren't sure what to make of it? Where would you take it?"

"Personally," he replied, "I'd take it to a friend of mine. He's sort of a 'shade tree' mechanic and his shop sure isn't fancy, but he really knows his stuff. He'd probably know immediately what's wrong with your truck."

"Then tow it there," I requested.

After towing our truck and trailer for nearly ten miles past McAllister and onto a narrow country road, the driver finally approached a repair shop at the edge of what appeared to be a small junk yard. A blackened cement building with garage doors at both ends was nearly blockaded by old car and truck bodies strewn here and there. As I peered into the dimly lit garage, I noticed a glow emanating from beneath an old truck. Looking more closely, I found a mechanic working there by the illumination of a grease-smeared trouble light.

After I told the mechanic what had happened to our truck and about its unusual noise, he asked me to start it again so he could hear it for himself. When I did, and as the "ka-chunk, ka-chunk" sound resonated from the engine, Richard (the mechanic) began flailing his arms excitedly, yelling, "Shut it off! Shut it off!"

He stood there just staring at the truck and remained quiet for a moment. Then he ominously declared, "Sounds like a broken crankshaft to me. Give me a few minutes to pull the oil pan and look inside just to make sure, but I'm almost certain that's what's wrong.

"Suppose it is," I asked. "What does that mean?"

"It means you'll have to replace the engine." he replied.

"And if I do, how much will it cost me?" I inquired further.

"Anything from five to fifteen thousand dollars, depending on what kind of engine you decide to replace it with," he answered.

It didn't take Richard long to remove the oil pan and ascertain that his prognosis was correct. Jagged pieces of metal lying in the bottom of the pan indicated that we did indeed have a broken crankshaft.

It would take several days, and would involve several thousand dollars, for Richard to replace the engine. Considering our options, we decided to have him replace it with a remanufactured engine. A remanufactured engine was cheaper than a new one, yet it came with a warranty which was almost as good.

Richard estimated, by the time his labor and shipping charges were added, that it would cost nearly nine thousand dollars. This was troubling news to us because for the past several years we had gotten into the habit of getting by on so little. Even though there were two families now, traveling in two separate rigs, we had experienced what we were calling "God's miracle of constant supply". Like the Hebrews traveling from Egypt to the promised land who's sandals and clothing didn't wear out in spite of forty years of usage (Nehemiah 9:21), we had experienced an unusual preservation of our equipment. It should have shown the usual wear and tear that constant travel and usage places upon things, but it didn't. We were somehow maintaining a perilous balance, on a financial tightrope, between our income and outgoing expenses. Now, because of our damaged engine, it appeared our tightrope was beginning to unravel.

Since we had meetings scheduled in Texas, we sent Jason, Laura, and Cami on down the road in their mini-home. They would hold the services without us while Karen and I remained with our truck until its repairs were complete. Richard cleared away the rubbish next to his garage and granted us permission to park our trailer there to live in while he worked on our truck.

On the following Saturday evening, as Richard was about to go home after working hard all day removing our old engine, he knocked on our door. When Karen answered it, he suggested, "I suppose you'll want to attend church somewhere tomorrow." Handing her a set of keys, he continued, "These are the keys to my Bronco. You may use it for transportation if you want to."

I didn't tell Richard that we didn't have nine thousand dollars to spend on a replacement engine when I commissioned him to work on our truck. We hoped that God would send along someone from somewhere to meet this need before the repairs were made. In the meantime, we had several days to spend, with little to do except to seek the Lord and pray.

It was easy for us to remain positive about God's promises of supply during the day as we poured ourselves into the Word, but at night when we tried to sleep, we were bombarded with negative imaginations of defeat, failure, and embarrassment. *We had barely met our expenses from day to day over these past few years,* I reasoned, in my sleepless state during the darkness of the night. *How could I expect God to supply nine thousand dollars within the next few hours?*

As the days went by and as Richard was getting close to completing the installation of the new engine, Karen and I found it harder and harder not to worry about how we were going to pay for everything. Our only source of consolation was the Bible's promises. During our time of study we noticed, particularly, how often the disciples used the "name of Jesus" in the New Testament. They seemed to use His "name", like someone uses a tool, to perform miracles. Peter and John, for example, healed a crippled man at the gate of

189

the temple (Acts 3:1—16) and then explained that it wasn't their holiness or power that caused this to happen, but it was "His (Jesus') name through faith in His name." We also noticed that names were often used in Biblical times to denote character or personal character qualities. Peter and John might have stated it this way; "The character of Jesus through faith in His character has given this man the strength to stand up and walk."

In the third chapter of Revelation, the church at Philadelphia had been commended by Jesus for "not denying His name". This suggested that they had continually exhibited the character of Christ and testified to it. Further study revealed that there are seven names ascribed to God in the Old Testament which reveal God's personal character qualities. These are: healer, provider, lord and banner, shepherd, righteousness, peace, and presence. Evidently the church at Philadelphia had not denied that God was their healer, provider, lord, and shepherd; or that He was their source of righteousness, peace, and faithfulness.

After working on our truck for almost a week, Richard told me the repairs were nearly complete and our truck should be ready the next day. That night, as I lay in bed during the early morning hours trying to get back to sleep, but tossing and turning instead, Karen recognized that I was awake. She told me she couldn't sleep either, but that God had spoken to her, inwardly, and had given us a warning, "Do not deny my name." He had told her. "Especially not at this moment. You can't afford to. Be especially careful that you don't deny my names of peace and provision."

When morning came, and the last few repairs were being made, I knew Richard would soon be expecting payment for his work. Not knowing what else to do, I called our bank in Nebraska and asked to speak to a loan officer.

"I doubt if you know me," I explained. "My name is Tom Cobb and I have a checking account at your bank. I've never asked to borrow money from you before, but the engine of our truck went out on us leaving us stranded here in McAllister, Oklahoma. I need nine thousand dollars to pay for its replacement, but I only have a couple of hundred dollars in my checking account."

The loan officer replied, "Tom Cobb? Sure I know you. You once held services at the church I attended when we were living in North Dakota. Nine thousand dollars for a new engine shouldn't be a problem. Go ahead and write the check and we'll cover it for you."

I wasn't sure what this meant, so I asked, "Don't you need some collateral first? Or shouldn't I sign some papers?"

"No, you don't need to," he replied. "Just fax us a copy of your truck's title and whenever you get home again you can come in and sign some papers for us then."

Although the balance in my checking account was only two hundred dollars at that moment, I made out a check to Richard's repair shop for the amount of nine thousand dollars. Assuming he would be cautious about accepting an out-of-state check, especially one that large, I wrote the phone number of my bank on a piece of paper, expecting him to call to make sure my account had sufficient funds to cover the check.

"No," Richard replied as he handed the paper back to me, "You seem honest enough. I'm sure your check is just fine."

In the months afterward, paying off the loan became a top priority for us. We experienced an unexplained increase in our income, and also a few financial "surprises" (an unexpected two thousand dollar rebate from the IRS, for example). After only nine months, we had repaid every cent.

Chapter Twenty Four

The Secret Place

Every summer, at Kadoka, South Dakota, former rodeo performers and some of the local cowboys, hold a rodeo Bible camp. Teens are offered instruction in the various events associated with rodeo by professional rodeo cowboys. These highly qualified instructors are not only able to help the teens improve their skills, but they also exhibit their own personal relationship with Jesus and impact them spiritually too. The camp at Kadoka is well-run and effective in its mission. Because of this, during one of the camps, we volunteered to help out wherever we could.

Jason served as a counselor to the boys. Karen and Laura helped in the kitchen. I helped drive the horses, calves, steers, and Brahma bulls into the chutes so the young performers could practice riding and roping them. We also provided music during the worship rallies which were held twice daily.

During this time, we became acquainted with Tony Shoulders. Tony was raised, almost from birth, to become a rodeo performer. His uncle, Jim Shoulders, had gained world-wide fame as a professional rodeo champion during the 1950's and '60's. Tony, himself, had an established reputation as a top contender in what many people consider to be the roughest event in the sport of rodeo — bull riding.

Because bull riding can be so dangerous, Tony was sharing with us how his students tended to become "religious" just before they mounted their bulls to make their ride.

"Some of them wear crosses around their necks," he told

us, "and use them as good luck charms, rubbing them in a special way. Others breathe a short prayer, promising God that they will do something virtuous later on to repay Him if He protects them.

"The problem is," he explained, "most of them don't follow through with their promises. Some of them become godly just before they make their ride, but then live like the devil until they get ready to make their next one. If they do get hurt, then they wonder why God didn't protect them."

Tony then quoted several verses from Psalm 91 — particularly the passages that deal with God's promises of protection.

Because thou hast made the Lord, which is my refuge, even the most high, thy habitation, there shall no evil befall you, neither shall any plague come nigh thy dwelling. For He shall give His angels charge over thee to keep thee in all thy ways, they shall bear thee up in their hands; lest thou dash thy foot against a stone. (Psalm 91:9—11)

What I'm trying to get these boys to see," he elaborated, "is these promises don't belong to just anyone. God made them especially for the people who dwell in His secret place. Most people don't know that such a place exists. Some people know about it and visit there once in awhile. But a visit to the secret place isn't enough. The secret place of God's protection is for the Christian who's made it his full-time dwelling place. It's not a place that we just visit once in awhile. It's a lifestyle. It's where we live."

Evidently Tony was successful in getting this message across. Shortly before the camp ended, nearly a dozen bull riding trainees prayed to receive Jesus as their Lord and Savior.

When we returned home, I stopped at the mailbox and picked up the pile of mail that had collected while we were

194

away. I noticed a letter from the Internal Revenue Service among the other letters and papers.

I wonder what they want? I thought to myself as I opened it.

To my shock, it was a demand for payment of eight thousand six hundred dollars in back-taxes. According to their records, I had made a serious error in a previous year's calculation of my taxes. I'd claimed deductions that didn't apply to my particular occupation and, therefore, I owed them all this money, plus interest — which was compounding rapidly on a daily basis. If I didn't send them a check immediately, I was warned, my situation would get much worse.

My last year's gross income had been only about twenty three thousand dollars. I was now sharing that income with Jason and Laura. How could I suddenly raise eighty-six hundred dollars? Worse still, if the IRS was right and I wasn't allowed these deductions, I would owe them similarly for other years because I had claimed the very same deductions since the time we had first started traveling. It seemed the federal government had the capability of shutting down our ministry.

The letter included two phone numbers that I could call if I had any questions or wanted to talk to an agent who would personally explain this discrepancy to me. I immediately called them, dialing the first number listed, but the only response was a recording, stating that "this number is no longer in service". I dialed the second number, but the line was busy. Throughout the afternoon, I stayed at my desk continually punching the automatic redial on my phone. Finally, at five o'clock the call went through. To my dismay an answering machine came on, informing me that the office was now closed and wouldn't reopen until nine o'clock the next morning.

The letter had come from an IRS office located in North Platte, Nebraska. We were already scheduled to travel through North Platte in a few days, so I decided to make an appearance at their office to see if I could talk to an actual person. In the meantime, I thought about what Tony had shared relating to Psalm 91. *Hadn't we been living in the "secret place" all of these years?* I asked myself. We had not only known about such a place, it had been our continual dwelling.

I also called our friend, Tom Elliott, to tell him about our tax problem. Tom's father was a CPA who had prepared our income taxes for us for many years and when he died, Tom (also a CPA) took on some of his father's former clients.

To my consternation, I didn't receive as much reassurance from Tom as I had expected.

"I think the IRS is wrong," Tom explained in a half-reassuring manner. "However, I can see where they're coming from. They don't think you should be able to deduct your travel expenses because you bring your living quarters with you. They probably compare you to someone like a construction worker who can't deduct his RV or the camper trailer he brings with him to the job-site because he lives in it while he is working on the job. No one is allowed to deduct the home he lives in unless special conditions apply."

My wife, who had been listening in on our conversation, countered. "But what about someone like Garth Brooks? You can't tell me he doesn't deduct his customized bus which he takes to his concerts, just because he may stay in it while he's on tour!"

"That's a good point." Tom responded. "I hope the IRS sees your situation as similar."

I had one more question: "What should we do if they

don't see it that way? Is there any way for us to get out of paying all this money?"

"If that happens, I think we should go to court. Tom replied. You may eventually get out of paying at least part of it,"

"Is there any chance of our getting out of paying all of it?" I asked, pressing for more reassurance.

I've never seen it happen," Tom answered. "Whenever the IRS is this confident about a case, they usually get something. And it's often a lot more than people care to pay."

On the day we'd planned to stop at North Platte to try and talk to an IRS agent, I stopped at our mailbox to pick up our mail. Inside was another letter from the IRS, similar in content and tone to the first one. This one informed me that I now owed the government an additional six hundred dollars.

Karen and I battled our fears toward this rapidly increasing threat by reading Psalm 91 and reminding ourselves that many years ago we had chosen to make our home in a secret place — one that hides us under the shadow of God's protection. Even if thousands should fall on either side of us, the Word had promised we would not be harmed.

Only a few months prior to this time, our country was shocked by news reports of the Federal Building in Oklahoma City being bombed and of hundreds of people, most of them government employees, being killed by the blast. When we entered the IRS office, the fear of further retaliation by a lunatic with a personal vendetta against the government seemed evident, even at the little IRS office in the close-knit community of North Platte, Nebraska. There wasn't a receptionist seated at a desk to greet us. Instead, on the wall of the small waiting room adjacent to a securely locked door was a button. Directly below it was a sign informing visitors that if they wanted to talk to someone inside, they should push the button. When I did, there was no response for a minute or two. Then I heard a voice from behind the door ask, "Who is it? What do you want?"

Sensing the tension, I explained the purpose of our visit in the most non-threatening manner I knew of and eventually a man opened the door and cautiously peered out at us. He apparently decided we posed no threat and ushered us into a small room piled with boxes and papers. On the opposite side of the room, a woman was seated at a desk, half hidden by the clutter. She was busily engrossed, poring over large piles of paper.

Without looking up, she spoke in a matter of fact tone, saying, "I'll get to you in a minute. Excuse the mess. Government cut-backs, you know. They can't afford to hire a secretary for me anymore."

As I waited patiently for her to finish what she was doing, I began to think, *Runaway government spending and excessive taxation has become a national concern. Citizens everywhere are demanding that cutbacks be made somewhere. But where? In education? No if the government were to cut its funding to the public school system, there would be an immediate outcry and politicians would probably lose their jobs. From Social Security? Again, it would be political suicide even to suggest such a thing. What about the IRS? What American citizen would care at all if anyone proposed cutting the funds specified for the IRS. Most of us, in fact, would cheerfully vote for whoever made such a proposal.*

Now that I had seen a human face behind this government force that had appeared so threatening, my fears quietly abated. I now felt pity for this poor woman who seemed to be drowning in a sea of bureaucratic paperwork. Eventually she finished her task and looked up, prepared to hear our complaint. My problems, however, didn't seem as important to me at the moment as hers did. I made an off-handed comment about the workload she seemed to be under. I genuinely felt sorry for her and she must have sensed it. Karen and I talked with her about her work for quite awhile, asking how she coped with its pressures and empathizing with her about the difficulties of trying to compensate for a diminishing budget. In the process, we nearly forgot about what had brought us to her office in the first place.

Suddenly remembering, I excused ourselves, saying, "Listen, I know you're very busy and we should let you get back to work. We're here today to see if it would be possible to set up an appointment with someone to discuss the additional taxes the IRS claims we owe."

This was done quickly. Before we left, she delineated for me which particular records and receipts I should bring with me to the audit, which might reinforce my position and help defuse the government's claims against me.

When we arrived home that afternoon, I called Tom Elliott and told him about the appointment we had set up with an auditor at North Platte. I wanted him to come along with us, as our representative, since he had prepared our tax returns and was much more qualified to answer the technical questions. Tom seemed happy to comply, but sounded concerned when I told him that we had already talked to an auditor and had briefly discussed our situation with her.

"That usually isn't such a good idea," he warned. "A person's first impression made upon an IRS agent often sets the tone for his or her aggressiveness when they handle your case. A representative, rather than the person whose livelihood is at stake, is usually in a much better position to make a positive first impression."

I suspect Tom was afraid we had already made things worse for ourselves by making first contact with the "enemy" with "our guns cocked and loaded", so to speak. To have done so would have been counterproductive to the good he hoped to accomplish on our behalf.

In Isaiah 65:24, there is a promise that states: "And it shall come to pass, that before they call, I will answer; and while they are yet speaking, I will hear..." I recognized a personal fulfillment of that promise when I began gathering my receipts, records, and accounting books in preparation for the audit. I've always tried to be thorough with my records, but for some reason I had been especially meticulous with the material dealing with that particular year. It was as if I had already been forewarned, two years beforehand, to make sure everything was neat, orderly, and accessible in preparation for when I would be audited.

One of the first comments made by the auditor, when the moment arrived that Tom Elliott, Karen, and I sat before her and I had placed my papers on her desk, was: "I see you've done a very good job of keeping your records organized and comprehensible. In fact, these are about the best I've ever seen."

As a preacher, there have been times when I've experienced God's "anointing" while preaching a message. The correct words just seem to flow, giving me the ability to quote obscure passages from the bible to accentuate my points — passages that I hardly knew. I was aware that God "anoints" preaching. But until the time of our audit, I had not experienced anything similar to it in the other activities of my life. However, while I as submitting my tax report before the auditor, I experienced a similar "anointing". Whenever she asked me to produce a particular receipt to coincide with and confirm my tax deductions, it always seemed to be ready for me at the top of my pile of papers. It was as if the angels had already sorted them in anticipation of her inquiry. After several such prompt responses, she quit asking me for special proof and appeared to trust the validity of my records as they were.

After her initial investigation, she picked up the telephone and placed a call to another office in Omaha to discuss my account with one of her coworkers. I didn't understand what her conversation was all about, but when it was finished she announced, "You won't be getting any more notices from the IRS demanding payment or interest on your taxes. I've just placed a freeze on your account so that no one from the IRS will be allowed to call or write to you for the next six months." Since I didn't understand why she did this, I didn't know if it was a good thing or if I was in serious trouble.

Eventually, she completed her investigation and began discussing with Tom the changes he should make when filling out my tax returns to keep us from being audited by the IRS in the future. From the grin on Tom's face, I suspected that things were favorable as far as our situation was concerned.

Finally, full of curiosity, I asked hesitatingly, "Does this mean that I don't owe the government ninety-two hundred dollars?"

To my immense relief the auditor chuckled as she replied, "No you don't owe the government anything." Then she added, "As a matter of fact, it looks like we'll be paying you about two thousand dollars."

As we left the auditor's office and were walking down the hall, Karen commented, "Well, that seemed to go pretty well, didn't it?"

Tom, with a stunned expression on his face, replied, "Lady, let me tell you something. It doesn't get any better than that!"

True to the auditor's word, we didn't receive any correspondence from the IRS for the next six months — no letters, no phone calls, and not even a post card. Then one day several months later, I received a check in the mail for twenty-three hundred dollars. An attached memo explained that this was money due us based on our amended return. Included in the payment was nearly two hundred dollars of added interest. Evidently, the six months "freeze", the auditor had placed on our account, prevented them from sending the payment earlier. They had added penalties and imposed interest upon themselves as compensation.

Chapter Twenty Five

I Am Not Afraid

Laura and Jason traveled with us and were our associates in the ministry for five years. During the second year, they had a baby, a little girl they named Jessica — our first grandchild. Needing more room, they sold their mini-home and replaced it with something more spacious — a thirty-two foot fifth-wheel trailer.

We shared our lives together, traveling from coast to coast, all across America and into eastern Canada. It was a special time and I hoped we would continue working together from then on, but one day they announced that they sensed a leading from the Lord to go back into the pastoral ministry. Perhaps to start a new Church somewhere.

Eventually, they started one at Chadron, Nebraska, but they also took a position as senior pastors at an already established church in Gordon, Nebraska. The church at Gordon would help support them, financially, while they began the new work at Chadron.

I spent several days praying and fasting to see if God was asking me to make some changes too. Perhaps I should consider taking a pastorate also and settle down in just one place. By this time, we'd been on the road for twenty-seven years. The denominational groups and most of the churches we had ministered to in the past didn't have special meetings as often as they used to and it wasn't as easy to fill our schedule anymore. Cami, our youngest daughter, was now a teenager and in a few more years she'd probably go off to college, like her older sisters had done, leaving Karen and me to carry on by ourselves. However, the more I prayed about it, the more I sensed God telling me that His calling hadn't changed. The gaps in our travel schedule didn't matter. If the familiar churches where we'd been before weren't interested in our ministry, then we'd take it to the streets. Somebody, somewhere, needed to hear our message.

*   *   *   *

A few weeks after we'd had the engine in our truck replaced at McAlister, Oklahoma, I'd noticed the belt that ran the hydraulic brake pump was frayed and showing wear. It shouldn't have worn out so quickly. Then a few weeks later when I checked the replacement belt, it looked just as bad. Something was causing an undue strain on the belts. I noticed the bracket holding the brake pump seemed out of kilter and surmised that this was probably why the belts wore out so quickly.

When I took the truck to a mechanic to have the pump repositioned, he told me the engine would have to be removed first, so the cast-iron bracket which held the pump could be heated and bent into proper alignment.

"There was a flaw in the casting of this engine when it was manufactured," the mechanic told me, "and the bracket is twisted. The only way to fix it is to heat it red hot and then bend it back into shape."

Pulling the engine involved a lot of labor and would cost hundreds of dollars. I chose to have the mechanic put in some adjustment shims instead, and try to align the pump that way. The shims helped a little, but they didn't solve the problem. Later, I took the truck to other, seemingly more qualified mechanics but, unless they pulled the engine, they couldn't fix it either. Finally, I decided I'd just have to get into the habit of checking on the belts every few days and replace them when I needed to.

Once, when we were traveling to Weippe, Idaho, I took our truck and trailer over a long winding narrow mountain highway. We had to go up a steep grade which continued on for about six miles — around switch-backs and alongside the edge of the mountain. There were no shoulders and very few places to pull over if, for some reason, you needed to. A few hundred yards before we reached the top, the brake belt broke. When it did, it whipped around and caught the radiator hose, ripping it apart. Steam and antifreeze from the hot engine began spewing everywhere and a dashboard warning signal sounded, telling me the brake pump wasn't working anymore. There was no place to pull over and I couldn't trust the brakes, so I had no other choice than to continue on up the hill, hoping the engine didn't overheat before we finally reached the top.

We made it, but it was a harrowing experience for all of us — one I didn't care to repeat. Karen wouldn't ride in the truck with me for the next mile or so after that, as we slowly made our way on to Weippe.

"I need to walk for awhile and settle my nerves," she explained. "I just can't get back into that truck again until I do."

A year or two later, we were invited to hold meetings at some churches in California and Oregon, so I'd lined up another tour to the West Coast. We would travel through Arizona and then hold services at San Diego, Fallbrook, McKinleyville, and Sacramento. After that, we were scheduled in Oregon, Washington, Idaho, and Montana. Our itinerary included travel through large cities and across numerous mountain ranges. I was pleased about the way the tour had been scheduled because the people had invited us and seemed excited about having us — and that didn't happen as much as it used to.

A few weeks before we'd planned to start the tour, Karen flatly announced, "I don't want to go!"

"You don't?" I asked. I was surprised because Karen was usually excited about going back on the road. She had developed a unique system for ministry, a few years prior to this time, that she really enjoyed. She would prepare a noon meal and then share Bible lessons with her guests while they ate. Karen is both an excellent cook and a gifted Bible teacher so usually, wherever she held her noontime Bible studies, they went over really well.

"Well actually, I do want to go." Karen explained hesitatingly. "I want to hold the meetings and I want to share with the people. I just don't want to ride in that truck back over those mountains again. It really scares me!"

Because I couldn't afford to buy a new truck, I didn't have many alternatives to offer her. Either we'd travel to the West Coast in the same rig we'd used before, or I would cancel the tour and we wouldn't go at all.

With mental images of our truck careening uncontrollably down a steep mountain grade, recalling some of our hair-raising experiences of the past, Karen began experiencing random panic attacks as the date of our departure grew near. To battle these attacks, she turned to her Bible. As she read it, one particular verse seemed to stand out. It was Deuteronomy 31:8:

And the Lord, he it is that doth go before thee; he will be with thee, he will not fail thee, neither forsake thee: fear not, neither be dismayed.

She memorized this verse and whenever she felt another panic attack coming on, she would repeat it to herself, out loud.

"God goes before me." she would say. "He'll be with me.

He will not fail me. I *will not* be afraid and I *will not* be dismayed!"

Karen counteracted her negative thoughts with these promises: *God already knows the route we'll be traveling,* she reasoned. *He's already been there and He'll clear the path before us. He will not forsake us and He will not fail us.*

Because of this, the panic attacks became less and less frequent. Eventually, she quit having them at all.

We started our tour and Karen remained calm and confident as we traversed the small mountain range between Arizona and California on our way to San Diego. After we'd held the services in San Diego and Fallbrook, the most direct route to our next destination was through Los Angeles — on Interstate 5.

Cami was taking high school algebra. Because she was home-schooled, her class room, on travel days, was the back seat of our truck. Karen was riding in the back with her, helping with an assignment, working on a difficult equation.

Typical of Los Angeles traffic, the traffic on Interstate 5 was bumper to bumper. An earlier traffic jam had been cleared and the cars in all six lanes were on the move again.

The vehicles were traveling a little too fast to suit me, perhaps because the motorists were trying to make up for lost time,. I was leery because of the unsolved problem with our brakes and wasn't comfortable traveling as fast as everyone else wanted to go. I kept my speed at about 65 mph as cars and trucks zipped around me, passing on both sides — most of them all in a line, bumper to bumper. Suddenly, as we topped the crest of a small hill, directly ahead of us was another traffic snarl. All the cars in all six lanes were stopped.

I slammed on the brakes, but the momentum of our

moving truck and our heavy forty-foot trailer impelled us forward. In spite of the truck's squealing tires and those on our trailer, we weren't stopping fast enough. We were about to ram, head-long, into the mass of stopped cars.

Karen began yelling, from the back seat, "God goes before me! He will not fail me! He does not forsake me! I am not afraid and I am not dismayed!"

To me, it sounded like a roar from the "Lion of Judah".

Jesus once suggested to the Pharisees that "out of the abundance of the heart the mouth speaketh." (Matthew 12:34) Often, when people find themselves facing an unexpected threat or danger, they will speak their fears and blurt out something like: "Oh dear! We're all going to die!" or at least, "Oh no! We're going to hit all those cars!" But Karen found the promises in Deuteronomy 31:8 more applicable and that's what she yelled out.

We were amazed at what we saw next. The pickup truck, which was directly in front of us, pulled over to the right side of the highway, and up onto a grass covered knoll. This gave us the added distance of the length of a vehicle to diminish our speed, but it still wasn't enough. Just as we were about to ram into the other cars, they began moving sideways — all of them in all six lanes. Some moved to the right and others to the left. They created an opening where I was able to bring our truck and trailer safely to a stop without hitting anyone.

When it was over, our rig was sitting astraddle of the yellow line. The vehicles around us on the six lane highway were now lined up seven abreast. Inside our truck, we all just sat there speechless for a minute or two. Then, Cami asked, "What just happened?"

Our experience must have been similar to Moses parting the Red Sea — except God did with automobiles for us what

He had done with water for Moses.

A week or two later, we had finished our meetings in California and Oregon and were now on our way to hold services near Olympia, Washington. As we passed through Portland, Oregon, we encountered road construction just north of the city. At one particular spot, the two outer lanes were closed and the traffic was funneled onto a detour bypassing a bridge. Long rows of cement barriers lined a makeshift roadway, forcing the traffic to merge into two lanes which were flanked by a concrete barricade.

As we rounded a corner, directly ahead of us, a pickup truck had stalled. Its occupants must have realized they were about to be "rear-ended" and had vaulted over the barrier to find a place of safety.

Having only seconds to react, I knew I didn't have enough distance to stop, so I chose to drive around the pickup in the other lane. I didn't have time to check my rear side-mirror to see if the lane was clear. I simply turned into it and skirted around the stalled vehicle.

The moment I turned back into the previous lane, a car whizzed by, honking its horn all the way. I didn't understand how it had been able to get around us so soon, since we'd just passed the stalled pickup.

Cami, who had seen everything from the back seat of our truck, explained how, "Dad, he was passing you at the same time you were passing the pickup,"

"But that's impossible." I replied. "There's no way three vehicles could pass, side by side, through an opening just two lanes wide."

I had been too busy concentrating on steering around the stalled pickup to see what was happening on the other side of our truck.

But Karen confirmed Cami's observation. "That's what

happened." she asserted. "I saw it too. He was passing you while you were driving around that pickup,"

*   *   *   *

I put up with our truck's faulty brake pump and worn brake belts for several years. One day I mentioned to my friend, Harley Schmidt that I had a problem with the brakes on my truck and no one had been able to solve it. Harley had once owned and operated a successful manufacturing company and Harley's particular talent was figuring out solutions to mechanical problems that no one else was able to solve.

"I can fix it." He announced confidently. "Let me have a look at it."

After making a quick inspection at the pump and the bracket which held it in place, he went to his work shop and created some new odd-looking shims. A few minutes later, he had them installed. After that, we didn't have any more problems with the brakes on our truck.

Chapter Twenty Six

Just Go!

It was lunch time and we hadn't stopped for hours, so I pulled off the interstate at the next rest area. We'd bought supplies for lunch at the grocery store the night before in anticipation of the long distances we'd be traveling. When we have a long way to go, and not much time between meetings, we often eat lunch in our trailer. So as soon as we parked, Karen, Cami, and I got out and stretched our legs.

Karen fixed sandwiches inside the trailer and as she sat them out, she commented, "I wish we'd have picked up some potato chips too, when we bought the lunchmeat last night."

The words were hardly out of her mouth when a Barrel O' Fun potato chip truck pulled into the plaza and parked right beside us.

Looking out the window, Karen saw the driver get out and walk toward the welcome center. Then she suggested to me, "Why don't you catch up to him and see if he'll sell us a bag of chips."

So I did. But when I asked about buying them, he told me, "I'm just a delivery man and not a sales person, so I'm not allowed to sell any of the Barrel O' Fun products I carry."

But then he added, "However, I'm also a company representative and I'm allowed to give free samples away if I choose to. My wife is with me and she'd like to see inside your RV. So I'll make a deal with you — I'll give you some chips if you'll give her a tour of your trailer."

I was surprised at his unusual offer but heartily agreed to

it. I ushered him and his wife into the trailer and began showing them around. She chatted away about their work and lifestyle and afterward, we shared some things with them about ours.

After our short visit, he went back to his truck and returned with a large cardboard box. Inside was an individual bag of every item Barrel O' Fun sold. He presented us with regular potato chips, barbequed potato chips, cheese curls, nacho chips, onion rings, and bags of items we didn't even know existed.

After they drove away and we sat down to enjoy the junk food smorgasbord we'd just been given, Karen made another comment, "Now I wish we had some soda pop to go with our chips and sandwiches."

At that very moment, a Pepsi Cola truck pulled up and parked in the very same spot that the Barrel O' Fun potato chip truck had just vacated. "Ooh Pepsis," Karen gushed. "Go see if he'll sell us a Pepsi."

I was already munching away, enjoying my sandwich and was so involved with my lunch that I didn't do it.

I should have been more aware. It was several months later, as I was praying and the events of that day came back to me, when I realized it had been more than just a coincidence for both trucks to have arrived exactly when they did. These were "set ups — those special moments, arranged by God, when we just "happen to be" in the right place at the right time. What happened to us that day wasn't just about potato chips and Pepsi. God used our desire for these things to bring us into contact with people who needed to hear our testimony and learn how much He loves and cares for them. The driver of the Pepsi truck may have needed to talk with us as much as the potato chip truck driver and his wife did — but I was too involved with my lunch to think about that.

*   *   *   *

After Cami graduated from High School and went off to college, Karen and I were left to continue on by ourselves. Our children had traveled with us for over thirty years. During that time, we'd always considered them to be an integral part of our ministry.

During our very first year of travel, for example, when Kiley was only three, we shared at a youth rally in southeastern Nebraska on a cold winter day in January. When the sun went down, the outside temperature dropped to below zero. We were traveling in our mini-home and were running late, arriving with only about two hours to get things set up before service time.

The first thing I'd planned, when we got there, was to take a quick shower in the mini-home. But when I turned on the faucet, the water lines were frozen. We had no water, but I also needed to shave, so I used a dry razor. That didn't work very well and I nicked myself in a several places. Placing tiny patches of tissue paper over the nicks to soak up the blood, I rushed outside to start hauling our equipment into the building.

We carried our keyboard and amplifiers in a small trailer pulled behind the mini-home. I went to unlock the trailer but couldn't find the key to the padlock. After wasting about ten minutes looking for it, I grabbed a nearby microphone stand and began pounding ferociously at the lock to break it off. Eventually, it came apart and I had access to our equipment, but my microphone stand was mangled.

I hauled the equipment in and set it up. The building filled with exuberant teenagers who seemed impatient because our program was late getting started. It had taken extra time to find a piece of bailing wire and attach the battered and unstable microphone stand to a leg on Karen's keyboard.

As we made our way onstage to begin the program, I tripped over a speaker cable which pulled the connection apart, leaving nothing but bare wires sticking out. It had to be fixed, so I ran back to the mini-home and got my soldering tools and repaired the broken cable while the teens waited even more impatiently.

Some of them probably thought we were a comedy team — me with tissue patches stuck all over my face (I had forgotten about them), and then stumbling around, falling over our equipment like a circus clown.

When the program finally started, Karen and I were so rattled we couldn't remember some of the words to our songs and important chords in our music. When I delivered the message, I got my sermon outline mixed up and forgot references to some of the Bible verses.

The only part of our program that seemed to go over was when I invited Kiley to sing *Jesus Loves Me.* Her performance, unlike ours had been, was calm and uplifting. In response, the teens yelled, and clapped, and stomped their feet to show their appreciation. When they did, it frightened little Kiley and she ran to me for reassurance, hoping she hadn't done something wrong.

At the close of our program, I offered an invitation (like Billy Graham would do in his Crusades), but I didn't expect anyone to respond. To my surprise, a few people actually came forward. One of them was a young muscular teenager named Dale.

In the years following, Dale went to Bible school and seminary and became a pastor. He was a success in the

214

pastoral ministry, affecting thousands of lives.

Years later, as we were visiting about that night in Nebraska when he made his decision to follow Christ, I asked him why he had done it. Our service had been so chaotic I couldn't imagine why anyone would have responded. Dale answered:

"To be honest, Tom — it was your daughter. When she came up and sang *Jesus Loves Me*, I thought to myself, *I want to have a family like that some day*. When I realized a relationship with Jesus could make that possible, I surrendered my life to Him."

*　*　*　*

We only had a couple of meetings scheduled for our upcoming Winter/Spring tour, so I was on the phone calling past acquaintances to see if their churches would be interested in having us back. Most of the calls I made were unsuccessful. For various reasons, the people I called weren't interested. I found it degrading asking for invitations, so I decided to spend a few days praying about it instead — before I called anyone else.

During that time, I sensed an inward directive from the Lord, based upon Genesis 12:1. God told Abram: *Get thee out of thy country, and from thy kindred, and from thy father's house, unto a land that I will show thee,* His directive to me, was similar. Abram was asked to leave his own country. My directive was to leave the things that had become familiar and comfortable for me. *My kindred* were the pastors and the special friends I had made over the years. I relied upon them to provide us with places to share our ministry, and they took up special offerings for us, so I was assured of an income. *My father's house* was my

215

denominational affiliation. I didn't have to deal with doctrinal issues, and few people disagreed with my concepts, as long as I preached to the people within my own denomination.

God told me: *Go back on the road with your travel itinerary left exactly as it is. Don't call any of your friends in the ministry asking them to let you hold meetings in their churches. Don't rely on your religious affiliation to connect you to people who may agree with your doctrine. Just go, and I'll provide for you.*

I was reluctant to do this for two reasons: What would we find to do out on the road with nothing scheduled? And how would we pay for it? I would have to go with nothing prearranged and nothing guaranteed. However, I reminded myself that if the just are supposed to live by faith (Hebrews 10:38), then that's what we should do.

In January, we held the three meetings I had previously scheduled, one in Kansas, one in Oklahoma, and one in Texas. After that, we had no idea where to go or what to do next.

We floundered around for the next week or two, staying at various RV parks and attending church services wherever we happened to be on Sunday. At one church, we interjected a few comments during a Sunday school class that drew attention to our ministry. Afterward, the pastor invited us to share in their Sunday night Bible study. We made new friends and had some interesting experiences in that community. Everywhere else we went, we weren't very successful at finding places to share our messages.

Then, because it was warmer in the South, we drove down to Houston, Texas and parked at an RV park there. On Sunday morning, I found a phone book and looked in the yellow pages to find a nearby church we could attend. One of the listings was only a few blocks away.

We drove to the address, but there didn't seem to be a church there. An old motel and a larger warehouse-looking building were sitting on the other side of a parking lot and a few cars were parked in front.

I pulled into the parking lot, intending to turn around and look somewhere else — assuming we'd gone to the wrong address. As I did, an old man with a long white beard stepped out from where the cars were parked and motioned for me to park alongside them. When he walked up to the window of my truck, I rolled it down slightly.

"I can show you where the sanctuary is, if you'd like." he suggested.

Karen and I obligingly got out and followed him into the building, down a long hallway, and through a door into a dimly lit room. A couple of tiffany lamps in a far away corner provided the only light in the room. As our eyes adjusted to the darkness, the first person we could make out was a thin-faced woman with tattoos everywhere — all over her face and arms. Another haggard-looking woman was standing beside her.

It all seemed so eerie. I glanced at Karen and noticed the *are you sure about this?* look on her face. I, in turn, tried to convey a *do you want to be the first to make a run for it, or should I?* look on my face. However, both of us just stood there, not sure what to do.

Then I heard singing from somewhere. The song was about Jesus. I thought to myself, *if these people are singing about Jesus they can't be too bad.* Giving Karen a nod of reassurance, I motioned for her to go on in and find us a place to sit.

Most of the people were at the altar praying. I followed Karen as she bravely walked up to the front, but instead of

217

finding a place to sit, she joined them at the altar. Different individuals led in prayer — and after awhile, Karen did too. Later on, I felt inspired to lead also. The service lasted for more than an hour. There was no preaching — only praise music, singing, and prayers.

When it was over and the lights were turned on, the people gathered around us asking, "Who are you? Where did you come from?"

We briefly introduced ourselves and then I asked, "What kind of a church is this?"

One of them answered, "This isn't a church. This is a prayer center. We also run a home for battered women in the motel next door."

Then someone asked, "So how did you find us?

"I saw your ad in the phone book." I answered. "I wrote down the address and followed it here."

"But our number isn't listed in the phone books —we're just a prayer center." I was informed. "You couldn't have found our address there."

I had no explanation to offer them, other than that God must have arranged it.

We learned that most of them were members of a Christian motorcycle club. Their leaders had once belonged to a street gang but they were now trying to reach their friends with the gospel

Karen and I aren't bikers, but they accepted us as if we were. They invited us to come back and share in their Tuesday evening service. The few we'd met with for prayer on Sunday morning invited their friends and we were surprised with the turnout. The building filled with people and Karen and I enjoyed an evening of worship and fellowship with our new (somewhat eccentric) friends.

The next day, we both had a feeling that we should move

on. With nothing to go by, except an inward leading that we needed to leave Houston, so we traveled on towards Beaumont.

After we'd driven for about an hour, we stopped at a rest area. As we were discussing what to do next, my cell phone rang. It was our friend Harley (the man who had fixed the brakes on our truck). He and his wife had a winter home near Naples, Florida and he had called to ask us to come down and spend some time with them — if we didn't have anything else going on. Karen and I considered the invitation for about a minute and then decided, why not? As long as we had no particular place to go, why not go to Florida?

When we arrived at Naples, I discovered that RV parks in that area were very expensive. Most of them charged more than twice what the going rates were at campgrounds further north. After shopping around, we parked at the cheapest one we could find.

When Sunday arrived, we attended an interdenominational worship service at the park's recreation building. We'd arrived about twenty minutes early so we visited briefly with the pastor before the start of the service. When we introduced ourselves, we mentioned that we had spent several years on the road as traveling ministers.

After the service was over, he called me aside. "I'll be in Honduras for the next two weeks on a mission trip and I need someone to preach for me while I'm gone. Would you be willing to do it?" he asked.

It had been less than two hours since we'd first met, so I was surprised that he'd offered his pulpit to me so readily. Realizing this was probably another "set-up", I told him I would.

That afternoon, the park manager called me into her

office to tell me that, earlier in the day, someone had stopped by and had prepaid our parking fees for the next month. Harley, our generous friend had taken it upon himself to help us.

We had been to Naples years before and had once held a meeting at a small church only few miles from the RV Park. They used to meet on Wednesday evenings for "family night", so we decided to drive over and see if they still did.

The church was open when we arrived, but only a handful of people were there. They'd had some issues with their pastor earlier that week, and in his anger he had resigned and walked out. Nobody was prepared to lead the service, so a layman read a few passages from the Bible and they began discussing them among themselves. Karen and I listened quietly for awhile, but we couldn't stay out of the conversation for very long. It wasn't our intention to take over, but we ended up dominating the discussion, sharing our opinions and concepts. The people didn't seem to mind and later on, they began asking all kinds of questions concerning the Bible and its application to life.

Later that evening, as we were still visiting, I mentioned Karen's noontime Bible studies and told them about her unique approach to sharing the gospel.

"Oh, that sounds interesting." One of them commented. Then he asked, "Do you suppose she'd be willing to hold a noontime Bible study here at our church?"

Karen readily agreed to do it. She would hold a noontime Bible study the next day at 12 o'clock.

When Karen spoke, the people seemed to receive her teaching enthusiastically. Consequently, they asked us to hold noontime Bible studies at their church on a daily basis.

One lady, in particular, commented about how much she enjoyed Karen's teaching and how she wished her husband could get in on it too. But, she explained, he had an incurable disease and hadn't been able to get out of bed for the past six months — except each week when she took him to the hospital for another blood transfusion. They lived less than a block from the church, but she felt it would be too difficult for her, and too hard on him, to bring him to the Bible studies.

One day she asked, "Would it be all right if we just prayed and asked God to touch my husband, so he'd be strong enough to attend these Bible studies."

I assured her that it would be perfectly acceptable to pray that way. The Bible study/luncheon was over, so those of us left in the building joined hands and prayed that God would touch him and he'd be able to come.

While we were still praying, I heard the door open and glanced up to see a stranger come walking into the room. The lady looked up also, and then gasped, exclaiming, "Steve! What in the world are you doing here?"

"Well," Steve answered. "All you've talked about for the past few days are these Bible studies. I was lying in bed wishing I could be here too. And then God touched me! So I got up, got dressed, and here I am!"

Karen held noontime Bible studies at the church for the next week and we experienced several miraculous and dramatic answers to our prayers. We had healings and breakthroughs of various kinds.

One of the men who'd become a regular attendant at the Bible studies called me one day.

"Could you use some bread?" He asked. "My daughter works at a bakery and sometimes they bake more bread than they can sell. I'll give some of it to you, if you'll take it.

"Sure." I replied. "Bring it on over.'

I expected him to bring us a loaf or two. Instead, he gave

us several dozen loaves. We didn't know what to do with all of it, so we set it on a table outside of our trailer. When people in the RV park walked by, we greeted them and gave them free loaves of bread. We made lots of friends that way. Every few days, our friend brought us more bread — boxes and boxes of it. Through this exposure — and because of the two Sundays we held worship services at the recreation center — we generated enough interest to begin holding Bible studies at the campground too.

Most of the people we ministered to were new converts (or people we hoped to convert), so I didn't ask them to take up offerings for us because I didn't want to give them the impression we were only there to cajole them out of their money. We didn't even ask them to pay for the meals Karen prepared and presented at the noontime Bible studies.

When we'd left home, we had about four thousand dollars in our bank account. After being on the road for three months, it was almost gone.

Lord, I prayed, *I am willing to go back on the road with no idea where we're going. I'm willing to minister where You have sent us. But we don't have a lot of money left. I think we have enough to get back to Nebraska. After that, I don't know how we'll live.*

Inwardly, I sensed the Lord telling me, *don't worry about it. You'll have more when you get home than you had before you left.* After that, I tried not to let it bother me.

When the "snowbirds" began leaving Florida, we decided it was time for us to go home too. As we were driving north, my cell phone rang and Karen answered it. It was one of our friends from Kansas.

"What have you guys been doing?" He asked. "For some reason, you've been on my mind a lot lately."

Karen told him about our faith adventure and how God

had led us to Florida and the ministry we'd found there.

In response, our friend stated, "You know what? I just inherited a bunch of money lately and I think God wants me to share some of it with you. He's been talking to me about this for quite awhile. So I'll be sending you a check for ten thousand dollars."

We received his check in the mail a few days later. God had answered my prayer. We actually had more money in our bank account when we got home, than there'd been before we left — a lot more.

Chapter Twenty Seven

My Father's Heart

Something that still bothered me after all the years we'd been in the ministry was my father's disapproval. He regretted the fact that I'd left the ranch to follow my calling and often expressed a desire that, one day, I would come back home and begin ranching again. I, on the other hand, prayed that he would, one day, have a "God encounter" and become a born-again Christian.

My father did things differently than most ranchers. Back in the 1950's when it became practical for cattleman to buy four-wheel drive pickups, horse trailers, and portable corrals to make their work easier, my father didn't do it. He continued using his team and wagon to get around the fences and if he had to ride horseback ten miles to get to a pasture to work the cattle, that's what he did. My father was tough, determined, and hard as nails. When I was a boy, he was my hero — I thought he could do anything.

I remember being about nine years old and camping at the "Kruger place". Dad had purchased a thousand-acre parcel of land about twenty miles up the river from the main ranch. The fences needed to be repaired so he hitched up his team and wagon, packed his tent and bed roll, and headed west. He intended to camp there until the fences were back in shape and he took my two older brothers and me along to help.

We pitched our tent along the banks of the Niobrara River next to a fresh-water spring. For a nine year old boy, this was heaven. I could swim in the river, explore the canyons, and best of all, Dad assigned me the job of being "camp cook". That meant I wouldn't have to accompany him and my brothers while they worked all day in the hot sun fixing fence. All I had to do was make sure the camp fire didn't go out and, just before they returned for lunch, I was supposed to put a bucket of water with a few cans of beans in it over the fire to cook.

I spent most of the morning swimming, except when I needed to add more wood to the fire. It had died down so I began gathering wood, hacking away with a hatchet on a cedar log along the riverbank. The sharp hatchet glanced off the log and hit my toe, causing a very deep gash — in fact I had nearly chopped my toe off.

I started crying for two reasons: it really hurt; plus, the accident would probably ruin our camping trip. It would take a half-day, with me riding in the back of my father's wagon, to reach civilization and the hospital

When my father returned to have lunch, I burst into tears as I told him what I had done. Rather than being upset though, Dad calmly inspected my bleeding toe, looking at it from various angles. Then he took a roll of toilet paper and carefully wrapped tissue around my toe — adding a few extra wraps for good measure. After that, he pulled a clean sock over the paper and told me to put my boot back on. "Don't take it off for three days." he ordered, as a final instruction.

That was the end of it. He ate his lunch, went back to work, and we remained camped along the river for three more days. When I finally came back home, my mother helped me pull off the boot and wash away the dried blood and toilet paper. By that time my toe had already reconnected itself quite nicely. I don't think she ever knew how serious my accident had been.

When Karen and I were first married, I worked with my

father on his ranch while I acquired a small herd of my own. At the same time, he helped me make a down-payment on a small ranch adjoining his. Even though I was now an adult, I still had a high regard for his wisdom and unorthodox ways of doing things. We worked together and seemed to get along pretty well.

When I left the ranch to go into the full-time ministry, he didn't understand why I would do such a thing. He blamed himself and often lamented, "I don't know what I did wrong. I never dreamed that one day I would have a preacher for a son!"

Dad thought I had gotten carried away with religion. I tried to explain that I wasn't following a religion instead I had found a relationship — a personal relationship with Jesus Christ. And rather than religious bondage, I had found more freedom even, than when we camped along the river or when I rode my horse across the open prairie.

I spent a lot of time pleading with God about my father's spiritual condition. I prayed over and over, "Dear God, would you save my Dad? Oh God, would you please save my father!"

One day I was praying that way and I sensed the Holy Spirit asking, "What do you want Me to do for your father?"

"Oh God," I replied, "Would you please save him?"

I was surprised when He asked, "How am I supposed to do that? If I sent Jesus back to the cross again, would that do it? Is that what is necessary?"

I was puzzled because I knew the atonement made by Jesus is sufficient for everyone, including my father. Then I heard God say, "I've already done everything necessary to save your father."

God wasn't telling me his situation was hopeless. Instead, He was telling me I needed to pray for my father in a different way. As I studied my Bible, I gained a clearer understanding about how to do this. *But if our gospel be hid, it is hid to them that are lost: in whom the god of this world hath blinded the minds of them which believe not, lest the light of the glorious gospel of Christ, which is the image of God, should shine unto them.* " (II Corinthians 4:3 & 4)

Then, in verse 6, I found a special promise, *For God who commanded light to shine out of darkness, hath shined in our hearts, to give the light of the knowledge of the glory of God in the face of Jesus Christ.*

From these verses I understood two things. First of all, God wasn't the problem as far as my father's salvation was concerned. Satan, the god of this world, was blinding his mind so he couldn't believe. Secondly, God places "light" (or understanding) into the hearts of those of us who do believe to reveal God's truth to unbelievers such as my father. When people finally comprehend what God has already done for them, they may choose, of their own volition, to accept Jesus.

After that, instead of continually asking God to save my father's soul, I began asking Him to show me how to make improvements on mine. I prayed, "Open the understanding of Your Word so clearly to me that I will be able to present the gospel in ways that people can't help but understand it."

Also, I began praying that God would place other dedicated Christians in his pathway and he'd be impressed by their Christ-like character and conduct.

It wasn't long before I recognized my prayers were being answered. It seemed that everywhere Dad went, he ran into dedicated believers.

One day he decided to drive his pickup from his ranch in Nebraska to my brother-in-law's ranch in South Dakota. Typical of his independent nature, he hadn't bothered to license the truck or buy insurance for it because he used it mostly for ranch work and hardly ever drove it to town or down the highway. However, a patrolman spotted him and pulled him over. It was then that Dad realized he'd forgotten to bring his driver's license with him. He had driven an unlicensed vehicle across the state line with no proof of ownership and without a driver's license. The officer politely escorted him to the nearest town and took him immediately before a judge.

The judge asked him what his name was, and when Dad told him, the judge responded. "Really? Are you any relation to Tom Cobb? Tom Cobb held some meetings at my church recently."

When my father admitted that I was his son, the judge seemed more interested in our relationship as father and son than with my Dad's lawlessness. He gave my father a brief reprimand, announced "Case closed!", and then invited Dad to join him for lunch. During the meal, the judge talked with my father about Jesus.

One of our neighbors had a seventeen year old daughter, named Carol, who worked in the hay field for my father during the summer. In spite of her youth, Carol had a bold faith in Jesus and shared her beliefs openly. Apparently, her testimony made such an impact on him that, one day, he asked her to promise to be there to pray for him when the time came for him to die.

"You know I can't promise that, Jack." Carol replied, "But I'll try to be there if I can."

Once, while we were on tour holding meetings in Idaho, I was given a message to call the emergency room at the hospital in Gordon, Nebraska, immediately.

"It's about your father." a nurse informed me. "If he wouldn't have been so stubborn, we probably could have saved him."

"What are you talking about? Is he dead?" I asked with trepidation.

"Not yet," she replied, "but I don't think there's any way he can live. His gall bladder has burst and he has poison all through his system. If only he'd come in a few days ago, this wouldn't have happened."

The thought of my father's imminent death prompted me to go into the church and pray. Years before, I had been reading Psalm 37:6. *And he shall bring forth thy righteousness as the light and thy judgment as the noonday.* Then I heard the Holy Spirit promise, t*he day will come when your father will acknowledge that you were right about serving Me all these years.*

Walking through the door, I began praying out loud, "My Dad *can't* die! Remember God, You told me that someday my father would acknowledge that I was right when I chose to leave the ranch and follow You ."

Suddenly, the next thing I knew, I was lying on my face on the floor. It was as if someone had jerked the rug out from under my feet. I remained there for several minutes making intense intercession for my father. Then the burden seemed to lift, so I started to get up to make my way on to the altar where I could pray on my knees in my usual position. But before I could stand up, I was back on the floor again experiencing the same heavy burden. Again, I felt relief and tried to stand, but I found myself back on the floor again, for the third time. This time, after several more minutes of agonizing intercession, I felt peace about my father and seemed to have an assurance that everything would be all right.

Later, when I told Karen about my strange experience, she commented, "Do you know what? Something very

230

similar just happened to me too, right here in our trailer."

Each of us had sensed a heavy spirit of intercession come over us with three distinct waves of intensity.

That afternoon, my mother called to tell me that the doctors had performed an operation and everything had gone very well. "In fact," She expressed with relief, "things are not nearly as bad as they first thought. Your father is going to be just fine!"

Weeks later, when we got home off tour, I told my brother about the abrupt message I had been given from the nurse in the emergency room. "Well — she was almost right." He commented. "Did you know that Dad died three times on the operating table?"

"What do you mean?" I asked.

"His heart monitor flat-lined three different times, but each time, he came back," my brother explained.

Sometimes I didn't think we were making any headway at all with him. Even his near brush with death didn't seem to change him. More years went by and he became an old man — eighty-nine years old, and yet he seemed as stubborn and independent as ever. I had now been praying for him for thirty-two years.

On a Sunday afternoon, a week before Christmas, Dad called to tell me, "I'm feeling some pain in my neck and jaw and I probably should go to see the doctor."

"OK, I'll be right over!" I responded.

My awareness of Dad's character made me suspicious. For him to *ask* to see the doctor probably meant he had a serious problem.

But Dad casually answered, "No, don't take me there today. I don't want to bother anyone on Sunday, but I'd appreciate it if you'd take me to the clinic tomorrow." Although I had my doubts about the wisdom of his decision,

I knew better than to argue.

When I stopped at his house the next morning, he appeared to be fine. I found him in the basement re-stoking the wood stove. He had just carried a twenty pound log in from the garage to the basement. He didn't seem to be having any problems so when we arrived at the clinic I left him in the waiting room so I could make a quick run downtown to pick up a few items we needed at home. About half an hour later, I was paged over the store's intercom. Someone from the hospital had called to relay a message. I was told that I was needed at the hospital's emergency room right away.

Trying to imagine what had happened, I rushed back and was relieved when I saw my father sitting calmly in a chair. He appeared to be all right. However, the doctor told me that he'd had a heart attack about three days ago and would probably have another one very soon. Things were so serious that they were having him taken by air ambulance to a hospital at Rapid City, South Dakota.

This was all foolishness, as far as Dad was concerned.

"They're just making a big fuss over nothing." He muttered. However, he went along with them and within a few hours he was resting comfortably in a bed at the Rapid City hospital. More tests were run and it was determined that he needed a quadruple by-pass. There was only one artery left supplying blood to his heart and even it was partially blocked. However, at his age, the doctor doubted that he could survive the operation.

His hospital stay lingered on for several days without much change in his condition while the doctors pondered their options.

On Christmas morning my sister called, telling me, "Dad had another heart attack last night and he's not going to make it this time. His lungs are full of fluid and his kidney's are shutting down. The doctor says he may die at any moment."

Karen and I returned to the hospital as quickly as we could. It was a three-hour trip from home so I prayed that God would keep him alive a little while longer. I wanted to talk to him at least one more time before he passed on into eternity.

Several family members had gathered in the waiting room to "say their goodbyes", but only two people were allowed in his room at one time so my wife and I went in together.

Shocked at seeing my father in such bad shape, I blurted out, "Dad, I'm not going to let you die!"

He responded weakly, "Well, nobody can live forever."

"Jack, there's one way you can," Karen suggested.

Although he seemed to understand, he didn't respond. He was in so much pain.

Claiming the promise found in Mark 16:18, *lay hands on the sick and they shall recover,* we prayed over him and then left the room.

Since everyone else seemed to be done talking with him, I was allowed to go back and be alone with him. I brought my Bible with me and immediately began praying that God would give me a promise from the Word to anchor my faith upon. I found it in I John 5:16. *"If any man see his brother sin a sin which is not unto death, he shall ask and he shall give him life for them that sin not unto death."*

I reasoned, *if my father dies without accepting Jesus as Lord, he will spend eternity in hell and no matter how much I pray, I'll never be able to bring him out of there.* But since he hasn't died yet, I'm asking for his life and God will give it because He's promised it to me.

A few minutes later a nurse entered the room to check

Dad's vital signs. Suddenly, she stepped back and exclaimed, "Well! Would you look at that!"

"What is it?" I asked.

"His catheter is filling up," she answered. "That means his kidneys are functioning again. In fact, they haven't worked this well since the day he first arrived!"

One of Dad's deathbed visitors was Carol, the neighbor girl who had helped him in the hayfield. More than twenty years had passed since he'd asked her to be with him when he died, but she hadn't forgotten. He was happy to see her and appreciated the fact that she'd come to Rapid City to keep her promise, but she was too late. He wasn't dying anymore.

The next morning, when they took an x-ray of his chest, his lungs were completely clear of fluid. A short while later he was released from intensive care.

One of the nurses exclaimed, as I pushed his wheel chair back to the recovery room, "I never dreamed I'd see him again. When they leave here in the shape he was in, they just never come back! I've never seen anything like this before!"

Because Dad had a reputation for being tough, some of his visiting friends ribbed him about how he'd endured the pain and was simply too tough to die. But Dad protested, "That's not what happened at all! I was dying, Tom and Karen prayed for me, and God healed me!"

Although I was grateful my father had been healed, I was frustrated because he still wasn't a Christian. I knew Dad was right, "nobody can live forever" — at least not without Jesus.

A few weeks later, we were in California holding meetings. I called our answering machine to retrieve its messages and one of them said, "Hello Tom, this is Carol. I thought you might like to know your father called me last night. He told me he had decided it was time for him to receive Jesus as his Savior. So I brought my pastor along and we prayed with him. Jack has accepted the Lord."

When I heard this, I forgot I was listening to a recorded message. Wanting to know more, I shouted into the receiver, "Really! Tell me what happened! Wow, Carol! This is great!"

When one of his friends asked him what had happened to him, Dad replied, "I finally came to the realization that Tom and Karen were right. And they've been right all along."

When he was released from the hospital, he went back to his ranch and finished breaking the workhorse colt he'd started working on before he'd had the heart attack. When he was 93, he turned the control of his ranch over to my brother, but he lived there for the rest of his life.

I really enjoyed getting to know the "new and improved" version of Jack Cobb — and he definitely was a changed man. He was 95 when he finally passed away.

The night before he died, I had an unusual dream. I was standing along the banks of the Niobrara River. I felt an urgency to cross the river and suddenly a beautiful white horse appeared which would take me there. However, there was no saddle or bridle on the horse, so I'd have to ride him bareback and trust him to carry me across without the use of a rein. The problem was, since there was no saddle, there wasn't a stirrup to step upon and I wasn't limber enough to swing up onto the horse without a stirrup. I needed someone to give me a boost — someone to help me get up on the horse. That's when I woke up.

Later that morning, I was informed that my father probably wouldn't live much longer, so I went to his bedside.

In his last hour, he repeated the Lord's Prayer and then he

prayed, "Let me die, Lord." But he still struggled away in agony, breathing, but not getting enough air — thirsty, yet choking when someone gave him a drink.

Finally, I said, "Dad, just get on that white horse and get on across the river."

It wasn't very long after that he died.

I suppose, when I meet Dad again in heaven, he'll say, "Thank you for helping me get on that white horse and across the river."

Or else he might ask, "Just before I died, you said something about a white horse. What was that all about?"

Chapter Twenty Eight

It's Too Hard!

"Mr. Cobb, my name is Virgil Lee and I-I'm calling to ask for your permission to ask Cami out on a d-date."

The person speaking to me on the phone sounded very nervous.

"You're what?" I asked, not sure what the call was all about.

"I want to date your daughter." Virgil repeated. "I'd like your approval before I do."

"Oh." I answered. Then after a brief hesitation, I added, "I guess that would be all right."

I'd met Virgil only a few times before. When we weren't on the road, Cami attended Wednesday night youth meetings with her friends Elisa and Rachel Wickman at the Victory Bible Church in Merriman — and that's where she'd gotten acquainted with Virgil.

Virgil came from a Sandhill ranch family. His great-great-grandfather, Old Jules Sandoz had settled in the Sandhills south of Gordon when the land had been parceled out to the homesteaders. Virgil's grandfather, Sonny Lee, had once worked for my father as a ranch hand. Virgil's parents raised Virgil to be a Christian. He attended high school at a Christian boarding school in South Dakota.

No matter what his background, when a young man calls and asks for your permission to date your eighteen-year-old daughter — how could anyone say "no" to that?

A few weeks later, Cami invited Virgil to attend church with us at Merriman. She played the electric bass with the church's worship team. I carried her amplifier in from the car and plugged it in, but it wouldn't turn on. I checked the outlet, the fuse, and the wires leading into the amplifier, but I couldn't get it to work. The service was about to start, so she borrowed someone else's amplifier.

We'd be going back on the road in a few days and I needed to have her amplifier working when we did. I could take it to an electrician, but the only one I knew of who could fix it lived over a hundred miles away and I didn't have enough time to take it to him.

Pastor Dave Morrison preached the evening message and closed it by asking, "Before we dismiss, is there anybody who needs prayer tonight?"

Dave often closed his services this way and it wasn't uncommon for people to come up to the front for special prayer. But that night, no one came. Just as Dave was about to close the service, I stood up.

"Something went wrong with our bass amplifier before the service started tonight." I informed him. "It's bound to be a big hassle getting it fixed before we go back out on the road. Would you join me and we'll just pray over it so it'll start working again."

Virgil had attended church almost every Sunday of his life, but he'd never been to a church where people prayed over their amplifiers before. *These people are weird.* He thought to himself.

Dave, however, was used to requests such as this and responded by saying, "OK, let's do it."

We laid our hands on the amplifier, Dave prayed a brief prayer, and then said, "Now turn it on and let's see how it works."

When I flipped the switch, the power light came on, the amplifier lit up, we plugged Cami's bass into it, and it worked fine.

It startled Virgil when he saw the amplifier come on. He told me later that he wasn't sure which frightened him more: being around people who would pray over their amplifiers, or the fact that when they did, it actually worked. He'd been taught that it was selfish and sacrilegious for Christians to ask God for things so trivial. Instead, we should submit to Him in faith, and graciously accept whatever life hands us.

Cami hadn't been brought up that way. She and Virgil continued dating in spite of their different theological backgrounds. They had some long serious discussions and, little by little, Virgil's concepts changed.

They were married the next year and Virgil and Cami moved to Scottsbluff, Nebraska where Virgil took a position as a youth pastor. The church offered the position to him with an understanding that they couldn't afford to pay him a salary. They would provide an apartment and the utilities would be paid, but he and Cami would have to have outside employment to make their living. Virgil began working as a car salesman and Cami got as job as a receptionist at the local YMCA.

They lived this way for over a year, and then Virgil called me one day. "Cami and I are quitting our jobs," he announced.

"What for?" I asked. "Why would you want to quit your jobs?"

"Because I've been called of God to be a youth pastor and I don't have enough time to sell cars and be there for the kids when they need me too." He answered. "I'm either called by God to be a youth pastor, or else I'm not. If I'm supposed to be a youth pastor, then God will supply my living while I'm at it.

"But lots of pastors work at two jobs." I protested. "The apostle Paul was a missionary but he also supplemented his income, once in awhile, by making tents."

"That's true." Virgil countered. "But in our case, a lot of the kids we work with come from broken homes. Some of them are really messed up and need lots of counseling. When they need me while I'm at work, I can't help them. Cami needs to be available too because the girls need a woman's counsel and I don't think it's proper for me, a guy, to spend so much time talking with teenage girls."

He'd made a viable point. Then he added, "A few of these kids have nobody to take care of them so they turn to drugs or they move in with their boyfriends because they don't know what else to do. I tell them, 'Accept Jesus. Turn your life over to God and He'll take care of you.' And they reply, 'So who does that? I don't have a job and I can't get one. How's God supposed to take care of somebody who can't even make a living?'

"I need to live by faith so I can answer, 'I do.' I need to be an example to these kids."

Still not convinced, I stated, "Virgil, nobody lives like that."

"You do." Virgil argued. "God does things for you all the time."

I had nothing more I could say.

Karen and I prayed fervently for Cami and Virgil. If this didn't work for them, it might do irreparable damage to their faith and their disappointment could destroy their ability to trust in God from then on.

About a month later, while we were driving down the road, my cell phone rang. Karen answered it, but we were just at the edge of our phone's signal range. There was some static, she heard Cami's voice, and the words, "It's too hard." After that, we lost the signal.

She immediately redialed Cami's number, but the signal

was too weak and the call didn't go through. She monitored the phone's signal meter for the next hour, hoping we'd drive into an area where we got a stronger signal, but we didn't.

When we reached our destination, I discovered that if I stood still in one particular spot, the call would go through.

When Cami answered, I asked, "What's going on? The only thing we heard you say before we lost the call was, 'it's too hard'. What's too hard?"

Cami replied, "I need to talk to Mom. I want to cook a roast but its frozen solid and it's too hard. I'm trying to thaw it out and I called to ask her, 'what's the best way to do that?'"

Virgil and Cami served the church in Scottsbluff as full-time youth pastors for the next eighteen months. God provided everything they needed in spite of them not having an outside income. They even made their monthly car payments on time. Afterward, God called them to Alva, Oklahoma, where they managed a Christian youth center and received a generous salary.

*   *   *   *

When we replaced our motor home with a new truck and trailer, in 1983, I had no idea we'd be driving the truck for the next twenty-five years. But when it was about five years old and it might have been practical to replace it, I'd been inspired by a passage in the Bible that said, *The rich ruleth over the poor and the borrower is servant to the lender* (Proverbs 22:7). God had already helped us get out of debt and I didn't want to borrow money to buy a new truck and go back into debt all over again. Also, I didn't want to make myself subservient to the banker and he could somehow influence the way we conducted our ministry.

The problem was, we weren't able to accumulate enough cash to buy a new truck. Whatever money we would set aside for that purpose was always spent on other more important things.

I serviced the engine regularly, took care of the necessary repairs, and we just kept driving it — always hopeful that perhaps soon, we'd be able to get a new truck. I did my best to keep it looking good and once in awhile, even when the truck was twenty years old, someone would ask us, "Is this a new truck?"

A horse trailer manufacturer had built it, so its body was crafted out of plate steel. It was durable, solid, and heavy — and practically indestructible. Once, when a motorist merged off the interstate, he sideswiped our truck's rear fender. The accident did significant damage to his car but it only put a small crease in our truck's fender — one I pounded out and repaired myself. Another time, a strong tornado-like wind blew down the building I had parked it in, directly on top of it. Other than put a small dent in the roof (which was easily repaired), it did no other damage at all. And, because the truck had kept the building from falling completely to the ground, it was able to be salvaged too.

The truck's odometer only went as high as 100,000 miles and then started over again at 0. I lost track, over the years, of the number of rotations it had made.

When we'd driven the truck at least 400,000 miles, and were on our way to hold some services at a church in Illinois, the clutch started giving us problems. We were traveling from eastern Indiana on our way to a town about seventy-five miles south of Chicago. I'd noticed the gears were harder to shift even before we'd arrived in Indiana, but they got worse as we made our way to Illinois. Whenever I let out the clutch, there would be a loud "clunk" and sometimes it took several attempts before the gears engaged.

We were within 60 miles of our destination, but it was starting to get dark, so we stopped for the night at an RV park. The next morning, just as we were getting ready to start out again,, our cell phone rang. It was John Wckman, one of our neighbors from home.

"What's happening with you guys?" John asked. "I've had a strong feeling for the past few hours that something's wrong and I should pray for you."

We told him about the trouble we'd been having with our clutch and that we still had 60 miles to go to get to our next destination.

"Ok then," John assured us, "I'll pray that your truck starts working and you'll get there without any more problems."

When I put the truck into gear, it shifted effortlessly. There was no grinding and no "clunk". Exactly as John had prayed, we drove the rest of the way into Illinois with no more problems. But when we pulled into town and were only a few blocks from the church, I shifted to a lower gear and heard the ominous "clunk" — it was back.

We were scheduled to spend only two nights at this church, and then we needed to be in Trinidad, Colorado (several hundred miles away) by the weekend. Since we still seemed to have a problem with our clutch, I shared with Karen my intentions. "We're supposed to be in Trinidad later this week and I don't have enough time to hunt up a mechanic and get our clutch fixed before then. Besides, it's been working fine today — up until now. I'm going to trust God to get us on to Trinidad and I'll try not to worry about the clutch.

We didn't mention anything about our truck when we held the service that evening. A farmer stopped by to visit the next morning. He'd been to our service the night before.

We talked for awhile and then he asked, "How's your truck working? Have you been having any trouble with it lately?

Since he'd asked, I told him about the "clunk" and how our neighbor had prayed for us, and that we'd driven the last 60 miles without any other problems.

"You know," the farmer suggested, "I have a hired man who is also a top-notch mechanic. I'd like to have him take a look at your truck, if you'll let him."

I agreed, and when the mechanic arrived, he listened as I started the engine and shifted the truck into gear. We heard an unmistakable "clunk" when I let out the clutch.

"I think the throw-out bearing's gone bad." He suggested.

The farmer drove it to his farm and the mechanic removed the transmission and dismantled the clutch. Then the farmer drove to Chicago to get the replacement parts. They worked all through the night so we'd be able to leave by 9:00 the next morning and make it to Colorado on time.

Before we left, I got out my checkbook to pay them, but the farmer told me to put it away, saying, "No, you don't owe us anything. Your truck's still under warranty."

I didn't understand. *How could our truck be under warranty? It had nearly a half-million miles on it.* Then I realized he was joking. However, he refused to accept any pay for all the work they'd done.

A month or two later, when the tour was over, we greeted our friends, John and Frances Wickman at church on Sunday. Mildred Denison had ridden with them. She was a widow who lived alone on her ranch a few miles away. Although she was elderly, Mildred had remained independent and self-sufficient. It seemed odd that she hadn't driven her pickup to church like she usually did.

When we asked her why she hadn't driven herself to

church, she explained, "My pickup is at the shop, so I asked John and Frances to bring me here today. The clutch went out on it."

When I was in town on the following Wednesday, I walked by the repair shop on my way to the post office and noticed Mildred's truck sitting outside.

Good, I thought to myself. *They must have Mildred's pickup fixed, or it wouldn't be sitting outside.*

Then I heard the Holy Spirit say, *go in and pay for it.*

We didn't have a lot of money in our account at the time, and my first thought was, *Can I afford to? I might have to borrow the money to do it.*

Then, after a moment of deliberation, I thought, *how could I not pay it? A month ago, someone fixed the clutch on my truck and wouldn't take any money at all. The least I could do, to show my gratitude, is pay for Mildred's clutch.*

Just then, Karen happened to be driving by in the car and stopped to pick me up. When I got in, I explained to her what I thought I'd heard the Holy Spirit ask of us, "I don't know if we have enough money in our account or not, but a few minutes ago, the Holy Spirit spoke to me and told me to pay for the repairs on Mildred's pickup."

When Karen heard this, she exclaimed, "Praise the Lord!"

"What are you so happy about?" I asked. "It might be pretty expensive."

She answered, "When we were in church last Sunday, God spoke to me about Mildred's pickup and said, 'take care of My widow'. I wanted to say something about it then, but I decided I'd wait and let God speak to you first."

I immediately went into the shop and told the mechanic, "I've come to pay Mildred's bill."

The mechanic got a calculator and figured up the total amount for the repairs. Then he suggested, "Since you're doing this, I'd like to help out too. If you'll pay for the parts, I won't charge you anything for the labor,"

The next Sunday, at church, Mildred testified, "I had to have my pickup fixed and I didn't know how in the world I would pay for it. But when I went in to talk to the mechanic about the bill, he told me it had already been paid."

After that, every so often, Mildred testified about how concerned she'd been when the clutch went out on her pickup. But God had assured her that He would provide — and He did.

Several months later, as she was retelling her story, she suddenly stopped in mid-sentence. Then, looking directly at me, she asked, "Tom, did you do it?"

What could I say? I couldn't lie to her, so I admitted that I'd paid for the replacement parts and the mechanic hadn't charged anything for his labor.

"I suspected that you might have done it." She stated smugly — as if she had finally solved a great mystery.

Chapter Twenty Nine

Overcomers

In Hebrews 5:13 & 14, the Bible states: *For every one that useth milk is unskillful in the word of righteousness: for he is a babe. But strong meat belongeth to them that are of full age, even those who by reason of use have their senses exercised to discern both good and evil.*

The phrase, *by reason of use,* might have been translated, *by habitual, or consistent use.* These verses imply that, through practice, believers may develop an ability to determine what is good and what is evil by no other means than through an inward directive from the Holy Spirit.

Over the years, Karen and I have tried to become more sensitive and more obedient to these inward directives. Whenever we both have a sense of the same leading, we've learned to be especially submissive to it.

We were in Salina, Kansas a few years ago and both of us had a feeling that we should start driving south.

When one of us gets an inward directive, such as we did that morning, we usually ask, "Are you getting the sense that God wants us to travel south today?" When both of us have corresponding feelings, we've learned to act upon them.

We began traveling south down Interstate 135, not sure what our destination was or how far south we should go. We hadn't been traveling very long when a semi-truck passed us and as he was going by, the driver motioned to me to turn on my CB radio.

The radio crackled and I heard, "Hey good buddy! I've been driving for quite awhile today and I'm gettin' kinda bored. I just want to talk to somebody. Where are you guys headed?"

"I'm not sure," I answered. "I think we're on a divine assignment."

"What do you mean?" He asked. "What's a divine assignment?"

I began telling him about the experiences we'd had over the years — about the Barrel O' Fun potato chip truck and about the time we almost lost our rig in Arizona, but a stranger kept it from rolling over the edge of the mountain.

We visited for the next hour or so. He seemed fascinated by my account of these experiences. He confided in me that he used to go to church but he'd gotten bored with it. He'd never had a "God encounter", like we'd had. In response, I shared my belief that God wants everyone to have "God encounters". A personal relationship with Him isn't only possible, it's an imperative.

Suddenly, I sensed the Holy Spirit telling me, *you've traveled far enough.* I told the semi-driver, "We need to turn off now, but before we go, would you like me to pray with you?"

"Would you?" he replied. "I'd really like that."

I prayed for him and as we parted, traveling in different directions, the last words I made out, as our signal broke up, was, "I promise you, when I get back home, I'll be in church next Sunday!"

*   *   *   *

Karen and I were invited to a cousin's wedding. The bride and groom were both elderly, each of them had been married before but had lost their spouses. It was a small ceremony with only a handful of guests so afterward, the groom invited everyone to meet at an exclusive restaurant and he would treat us to a gourmet meal.

A long table was set up in a corner for the wedding party, but other patrons were eating their meals at tables scattered around the room too. The waiter happened to seat Karen and me directly across from the newlyweds.

Making conversation, Karen's cousin asked, "You and Karen have been traveling and holding meetings for quite a few years now. How do you do it? How do you get scheduled? Do you hire an agent who sets things up for you?"

"No," I replied. And then to cite an example, I told her about the experience we'd had with our motor home and how a stranger found the tire we needed lying in a ditch along the side of the road. We both were in the right places at the right time and God supplied exactly what we needed.

"After that encounter," I explained, "Whenever we're traveling through that area, his church invites us back to hold services for them."

I was engrossed, telling my story, and didn't realize that while I was talking, eavesdroppers were listening. When I stopped speaking, I became aware of the silence. Everyone in the restaurant had become quiet, waiting to hear the outcome of my story.

*   *   *   *

For our fortieth wedding anniversary, our children sent us on a five-day cruise from Galveston, Texas to the Yucatan peninsula.

When we boarded, I hoped we would meet fellow believers — people Karen and I would enjoy getting acquainted with. Although I looked around, nobody stood out. If there were any committed Christians on the ship, none of them acted like it. I thought of what Jesus warned His disciples about when He described the "last days". People would be eating, and drinking, marrying and giving in marriage. I thought to myself, *that's what people do when they go on a cruise. They eat, they drink, they marry, or they try to find somebody else to marry.*

I began mingling with the passengers and through our conversations, I determined that some of them were lonely, a few were depressed, and most of them were disillusioned — not too hopeful about the future. I didn't force anyone to listen to my testimony, but through casual conversations I found opportunities to share my stories, and most of the people I talked to seemed to be impacted by them.

When we'd been on the boat a couple of days, we met another couple who were committed Christians. We enjoyed swapping stories with each other, telling about God's miraculous ways of deliverance and provision. Once, when we were visiting, eavesdroppers began picking up on our conversation. There must have been a hundred people in the same room, and one by one, they became silent and leaned in to hear what we were saying. No one interrupted us. No one argued with us or scoffed at us. One lady got up to leave, but as she walked by, she patted me on the shoulder, winked at me, and whispered, "Good job!" She must have been a believer too.

*   *   *   *

Once, when Karen and I were in the checkout line at a grocery store, I looked at the sales clerk and suddenly got weak in the knees. As soon as we were outside, I told Karen why I'd been so shaken.

"I don't know what I'm supposed to do." I informed her.

"I'm certain I've never seen that check-out lady before in my entire life. But I recognize her. I had a dream last night and she was in it!"

Karen considered my dilemma and then advised, "This is a 'God thing'. God must have something He wants you to share with that lady. You need to go back into the store and talk to her."

I went back hoping she'd be taking a break, or at least to find her without any customers so I could talk with her privately. But that didn't happen. It seemed as if everyone in the building had all decided to check out at the same time. Long lines of people stood behind the half-dozen registers which were open and more sales clerks were called up to the front to take care of the sudden influx of customers. I took a place at the end of the line at her counter and waited my turn.

While I was standing there, I began thinking, *how do I do this? What will I say to her? It certainly wouldn't work if I came up and said, "Hey babe, I saw you in my dreams last night."*

She was a nice looking lady, so I'd have to be subtle or else she might think I was a reprobate trying to make a pass at her.

I was still busy trying to decide what to say when I realized I was next in line and it was my turn. I just stood there for a moment while she looked at me, puzzled because I hadn't placed any items on her counter.

Finally, I blurted out, "I'm not a kook!" Then as I gained some composure, I explained. "As a matter of fact, I'm a preacher. I know we've never met before but I saw you in my dream last night. Only in my dream, you weren't a check-out lady, you were a doctor. Is there anything significant about that?"

Everyone within earshot of us became quiet. Even the

beeps and clicks from the adjacent cash registers faded away into silence.

The lady just stared at me, not saying anything. Finally, the clerk at the next register offered a suggestion, "Sally, what about your husband? Would this have anything to do with him?"

At this, Sally began crying. Then, wiping her eyes, she explained. "Yes, my husband just left me. I would like him to come back, but I don't want him if he doesn't want to be back."

There was a long line of people at Sally's counter still waiting to check out and I realized I would be imposing on them, and might get Sally into trouble, if I talked with her for very long. However, before I left, I assured her that I would be praying for her.

I believe that her being a doctor in my dream, symbolized her capability of healing their broken relationship. She was the doctor, as far as the restoration of their marriage was concerned. That was the message God wanted me to share with her.

Although it was awkward for me, I was happy to be used of God as one of His messengers.

The Bible, when describing the battle between believers and the devil, tells us, *they overcame him by the blood of the Lamb and by the word of their testimony.* (Revelation 12:11)

I find it interesting that along with "the blood of the Lamb", "the word of our testimony" is also used to defeat the devil. Christians, over the centuries, have recognized the power of "the blood" and use it gain victory over the world, the flesh, and the devil. However, there hasn't been as much emphasis placed upon "the Word of our testimony".

Therefore, whenever I share my testimony, I try to include the Word in it. When I speak to people, I tell them the Scriptures I stand upon and point them to the promises found in the Bible which I've used as the foundation for my prayers. I believe the same "Word" that causes me to "overcome" is capable of producing positive results for other people too.

That's what motivated me to write this book.